A Soviet Lexicon

A Soviet Lexicon

Important Concepts, Terms, and Phrases

Roy D. Laird
Betty A. Laird

Lexington Books
D.C. Heath and Company/Lexington, Massachusetts/Toronto

Library of Congress Cataloging-in-Publication Data

Laird, Roy D.
A Soviet lexicon.

Bibliography: p.
1. Soviet Union--Politics and government--
1917- --Terminology. I. Laird, Betty A. II. Title.
DK266.3.L27 1988 947.084 87-45571
ISBN 0-669-16738-X (alk. paper)
ISBN 0-669-16739-8 (pbk. : alk. paper)

Published simultaneously in Canada
Printed in the United States of America
Casebound International Standard Book Number: 0-669-16738-X
Paperbound International Standard Book Number: 0-669-16739-8
Library of Congress Catalog Card Number: 87-45571

The paper used in this publication meets the minimum requirements of American National Standard for Information Sciences—Permanence of Paper for Printed Library Materials, ANSI Z39.48-1984. ∞™

88 89 90 91 92 8 7 6 5 4 3 2 1

To those students at the University of Kansas whose questions and answers (on the "objective" part of the Laird exams) over more than three decades provided the stimulus for the Lexicon.

Contents

Acknowledgments ix

Introduction **1**
Why a Lexicon?
What Has Been Included, and What Excluded?
Using the Lexicon
Notes

The Soviet System: A Brief Introductory Sketch **9**
Roots of the System: Geographic and Historical Factors
The House That Stalin Built
Conclusion: Avoiding Mirror-imaging
Note
Selected Monographs

The Lexicon **35**

Appendix 1: Full and Candidate Members of the Politburo: 1917–87 114

Appendix 2: The Constitution (Fundamental Law) of the Union of Soviet Socialist Republics 139

Appendix 3: The Rules of the Communist Party of the Soviet Union 179

About the Authors

Acknowledgments

WE ARE enormously indebted to the legion of Sovietologists and their many books that were consulted in preparing the definitions offered here. We are especially grateful to the Munich-based researchers in the former Institute for the Study of the USSR, and those now at RFE/RL, whose research made possible the biographical sketches of Soviet political leaders (past and present) that appear in appendix 1. Most of all, we are indebted to Alan Holiman, M.A., Professor William Fletcher of the University of Kansas; Dr. Peter Shearman of Essex University; Professor Darrell P. Hammer of the University of Indiana; Professor George E. Hudson of Wittenberg University; and Dr. Jacob Kipp and Lt. Col. Bob Stockwell of Fort Leavenworth, Kansas. Each of them read, and sometimes reread, the manuscript in at least one of its various drafts, and made many valuable changes and additions. Finally, the University of Kansas is a superb base for producing such work. Of course, all the faults are our responsibility.

Introduction

[Russia] is a riddle wrapped in a mystery inside an enigma.

Winston S. Churchill
Radio broadcast
1 October 1939

Why a Lexicon?

This book is designed to provide a basic understanding of the words, concepts, and phrases essential to interpreting the Soviet system, its politics and economics, its problems, successes, failures, and goals.

In almost any realm of study, comprehension of the subject depends first and foremost upon a familiarity with the basic terminology. For example, in the beginning, the chemistry student must learn the various symbols for the elements as presented in the periodic table. Of course, memorizing all the symbols, let alone the characteristics of the elements (their weights, positions in the table, and valences) may take months, indeed, years. Therefore, the periodic table and a more comprehensive manual are kept at hand for quick reference. The authors believe that this lexicon will serve as a unique manual for those wishing to expand their knowledge of Soviet affairs, particularly in the political, economic, and social realms.[1]

Unfortunately, unlike the hard sciences, the social sciences have no universal language. Specifically, there is no common understanding of terms accepted by all who study and interpret Soviet affairs. Quite to the contrary, there are profound differences, even over such seemingly basic concepts as democracy and freedom. As a result, there is often a breakdown in communication.

In the discourse on Soviet affairs there are three different vocabularies: (1) definitions used by analysts, such as the authors, that are not shared by adherents to Marxist-Leninist doctrine; (2) Soviet connotations of terms (shared by Marxist-Leninists outside the USSR) that are rejected by most non-Marxist-Leninist commentators; and (3) universal connotations used by most knowledgeable individuals whatever their ideological persuasions.

In the babel of cross-cultural discourse the words used may appear to be the same, may even be spelled the same way, but may often have meanings that are fundamentally different. Therefore, whether read in the original Russian or in translation, any message from a Soviet writer is understandable to U.S. or European readers only to the degree that the latter are aware of the Soviet writer's lexicon of terms.

Some of the difficulty in Soviet–U.S. communication rests in semantics, a problem that goes well beyond language differences. Important variations in connotation and/or use that muddy the waters of communication can be illustrated by examples of definitions and explanations included in the body of the *Lexicon*.

bourgeois objectivism An accusation leveled at intellectuals, in all branches of learning, who do not follow the party line in the "ideological rearmament" of the Soviet peoples. Such intellectuals are accused of being apolitical or harmfully objective in their viewpoint and analysis.

Czech Spring A Western description for the ill-fated period of Czechoslovakian reform and revitalization in 1968 that was ended by Soviet and Warsaw Pact military intervention. That intervention heralded the establishment of the **Brezhnev Doctrine,** which see.

democracy "Socialist democracy is the only genuine democracy." In Marxist-Leninist theory, there is no democracy except under communism. The emphasis is on equality—especially economic equality, which is defined as all having the same relationship to the means of production. See **freedom.**

elections Although the USSR has local and national balloting for state offices, before Gorbachev's rise to power, only one candidate ever appeared on the ballot for each office, and that individual had to be approved by the party. Beginning in 1987 there have been some instances of multiple candidates at the local level. Election day is a national holiday. Voter turnout is very high because elections are a form of political participation and a legitimizing device; thus, going to the polls is the proper thing to do.

Finlandization A Western term applied to the political neutralization of Finland. The term describes any country that accedes, especially in the foreign policy realm, to Soviet desires.

freedom "The perception of necessity" is a phrase used repeatedly by Soviet political philosophers. According to Soviet doctrine, one can be free only if one behaves according to the dictates of the Marxist-Leninist "science of society." Therefore, freedom consists of acknowledging those dictates and choosing to follow them.

propaganda Selected information and admonishments directed at the masses to train them in Marxist theory and to direct them toward Soviet goals. In the USSR the term "propaganda" does not have negative connotations. Indeed, it is an integral part of the communications media and the educational system to effect mass mobilization. See **agitprop.**

Unaware of Soviet definitions and practices, an outsider may read, for example, that an election has been held in the USSR and falsely assume that Soviet voters select their political leaders. As informed individuals know (and this emphatically includes Soviet citizens), all important posts in the USSR (whether they are filled by election or appointment) are filled by the party exercising its "right to control." Thus, employing the nomenklatura (party lists of individuals deemed worthy of filling the office in question), the party nominates all candidates whose names go on the ballot.

Aware of the special Soviet lexicon, a knowledgeable American who reads a quotation from a speech by Gorbachev stating that he is in favor of using propaganda to further democracy and freedom will understand that what Gorbachev was saying to his Soviet listeners is that all means of persuasion should be used to promote equal relationships to the means of production and maximum adherence to the "scientific laws of Marxism-Leninism." Without a knowledge of the Soviet lexicon, a totally different message would be conveyed.

For the seasoned Western Soviet specialist, there will be little or nothing new in the pages that follow. Indeed, undoubtedly some will disagree with the wording of some of the definitions and explanations offered. However, we ask our colleagues to remember how meager their knowledge was when they were beginners in the field, to recognize the usefulness to students and nonspecialists of such a reference, and to acknowledge the impossibility of pleasing all members of their fraternity.

Having stated what we believe this book to be, we also must stress what it *is not.* Given both the limits of space and individual connotation, no single entry or explanation presented in these pages is meant to be fully definitive. Indeed, whole books have been written on many of the terms listed. If properly used, this book will provide the user with an initial introduction to unfamiliar words and phrases, though not with the full meaning, history, or connotation of any term or event. Complete understanding may require extensive reading and research. For example, whereas our identification of some of the essential elements of Stalinism surely is correct, anyone wanting fully to understand Stalin's impact during his three decades as the supreme leader of the USSR will have to digest several volumes of literature and analysis.

What Has Been Included, and What Excluded?

What has been included stems largely from nearly forty years of specializing in the Soviet field and listening to students' questions. Thus, most of what is offered here constitutes brief answers to the queries raised. In that connection, the transliteration of Russian terms and the translation of phrases used in Soviet discourse are those that the reader will encounter in English-language books, articles, and newspaper reports on Soviet affairs. Thus they have become a part of the vocabulary of Western Soviet studies. For example, kolkhoz and chernozem are used by many Western writers rather than their English equivalents, collective farm and black earth.

What has not been included? With a few exceptions (for example, Siberia and tundra), we have not included geographical place names and terms. Geography texts tend to be quite complete, with glossaries, indexes, maps, and other graphic presentations that do not belong in this book. With a few exceptions, there has been no attempt to include the names of prominent Soviet personalities outside the Politburo. Their names are too many, and other reference books present the biographies in a much more complete form than could be offered here.[2] The major exception has been entries for those individuals whose actions resulted in their names becoming a part of the lexicon of discourse—for example, Lysenkoism and Zhdanovism. The most difficult decisions regarding inclusion or exclusion had to do with concepts, events, and terms that originated before 1917. Without any doubt, had we approached the task from the perspective of a student of Russian *and* Soviet history (even though the work was intended to concentrate on the contemporary Soviet scene), many more items associated with the pre-Soviet period would have been included.

Clearly, our approach is only one of many possibilities, and it reflects our priorities and prejudices. However, any attempt to expand such a volume to include every perspective and nuance of meaning would destroy the volume's usefulness as a convenient, quick reference. Therefore, we offer the *Lexicon* as a beginners' tool, assuming that anyone serious about increasing his or her knowledge about the USSR will consult more specific and detailed works.

Using the Lexicon

The newcomer to the study of the Soviet Union may encounter the word *transliteration* for the first time. This term refers to the conversion of Russian words spelled in the Cyrillic alphabet into Russian words spelled in the Roman alphabet, making them more intelligible to English-speaking people.

Because there are a number of letters in the Cyrillic alphabet that have no equivalent in the Roman, there may be several ways of transliterating a single Russian letter. None of the standard systems of transliteration seems to be entirely satisfactory. For the *Lexicon,* the authors have generally chosen to use the Library of Congress system without diacritical markings. However, the reader will find some exceptions, such as Russian words and names that have a common spelling in English: Trotsky (rather than Trotskii); Soviet (rather than Sovet); Moscow (rather than Moskva); and Politburo (rather than Politbiuro). Also, the names in appendix 1 generally follow the spellings used by the original Munich researchers who created the *Who's Who* biographies from which the information was taken.

Where appropriate, both the transliterated Russian terms and the English terms are supplied. In such cases the user is referred to the English term—for example, "**glasnost** See **openness.**" Quotation marks are used for three purposes: (1) to indicate a quotation or slogan; (2) to suggest that the Soviet meaning of a term may differ significantly from Western usage—"elected" is to remind the reader that what are called elections in the USSR are very different from elections in the West; and (3) to indicate that the definition or explanation given is from the Soviet point of view, and thus the connotation is not one employed by most Westerners—for example, **freedom** "The perception of necessity."

Notes

1. There are three other valuable reference works that, though somewhat similar to the *Lexicon,* do not fully serve its purpose. This work is unique for two reasons. As explained in detail in the introduction, we have attempted to include as many terms and concepts as possible that are likely to be new to the nonspecialist or that, although they may appear familiar, have a special connotation when applied to Soviet affairs. Further, the definitions and explanations presented have been deliberately kept as brief as possible because a major goal was to provide a quick, introductory reference.

The three references consulted in producing this work are:

Barbara P. McCrea, Jack C. Plano, and George Klein. *The Soviet and East European Political Dictionary.* Santa Barbara, Ca., and Oxford, England: ABC Clio Information Series, 1984. A major strength of this work is that most of the terms and concepts covered are discussed in considerable depth, that is, often several pages are devoted to a single entry.

Raymond S. Sleeper, ed. *A Lexicon of Marxist-Leninist Semantics.* Alexandria, Va.: Western Goals, 1983. The major value of this book is that most of the entries are devoted to direct quotations from Soviet leaders and the Soviet press.

S. V. Utechin. *Everyman's Concise Encyclopaedia of Russia.* London and New York: J. M. Dent & Sons Ltd, and E. P. Dutton & Co. Inc., 1961. Although now somewhat dated, this is still an extremely valuable reference, especially strong on history, prominent personalities, and geographical facts.

2. The Munich-based scholars and researchers, associated with the former Institute for the Study of the USSR and now with RFE/RL, have produced by far the most exhaustive biographies of prominent Soviet individuals. Their invaluable volumes include *Who Is Who in the USSR, Who Was Who in the USSR, Prominent Soviet Personalities in the USSR,* and the more recent compilations by Alexander G. Rahr, *A Biographic Directory of 100 Leading Soviet Officials.*

The Soviet System: A Brief Introductory Sketch

We the leaders are responsible for everything. Therefore, we must understand everything, recognizing right from wrong, and good from evil, supporting the right way and vanquishing the wrong way.

Nikita S. Khrushchev
Speech to agricultural workers
1957

WHOLE VOLUMES are needed to describe the Soviet system in all of its complexity. Thus, the few pages that follow are far from a comprehensive description of the Soviet economic, political, and social scene. What we hope the material provides is a thumbnail sketch of some of the more essential features of the Soviet system that will help the beginner better understand the entries in the *Lexicon* and spur him or her on to further study. For the latter reason, a list of a few of the most recent surveys of Soviet affairs is offered at the end of the chapter.

Roots of the System: Geographic and Historical Factors

Although a new leadership may attempt to impose radical changes in a nation, as did the Bolshevik leaders at the beginning of the Soviet system in 1917–18, they cannot escape their environment, particularly the history of that nation and its geography. Thus, the Soviet system cannot be understood without a knowledge of tsarist history and the human and natural resources and special features of the part of the Eurasian continent that constituted the tsarist empire.

Geography and Natural Resources

The geographic factors and forces that helped shape tsarist Russia and that now influence the Union of Soviet Socialist Republics are enormously important, both in terms of opportunities offered and limitations imposed.

The USSR is by far the largest country in the world, nearly three times the size of our contiguous forty-eight states. From the western land boundaries to the eastern coastal tip in the Bering Strait, there are eleven time zones.

Agriculture is the largest single segment of the economy. The area sown to crops is immense, much larger than that in the United States. However, the location of the vast majority of Soviet farms is not conducive to high crop yields.

Some one-third of the Soviet land mass lies in the northern permafrost zone. That region is not suited to cultivation. Although there are areas where the sun-loving crop cotton is grown in the south, most Soviet farmland is faced with long, hard winters and short, hot summers. Associated with that fact are two unfavorable factors as far as crops are concerned. Periodically, in much of the farming area, winter kill (because of extremely cold winters coinciding with inadequate snow cover) seriously reduces yields of grain planted in the autumn. Also, because the growing season is so short, often crop yields are reduced by late spring or early fall frosts and/or untimely precipitation (sometimes snow) that disrupts planting and harvesting.

Finally, there is the problem of frequent drought over large areas. Even in normal years the major part of the Soviet farming area receives less than eighteen inches of precipitation a year. Thus, much of the land is marginal for growing grain (by far the most important crop), especially because the precipitation that does fall often does not occur at the most propitious time. As a result, Soviet grain production varies widely from year to year. Often there is a widespread crop failure which, in the past, resulted in famines that have punctuated both tsarist and Soviet history. Only since Khrushchev's rule (1953–64) has famine disappeared, in large part because the USSR has stopped being a major grain exporter and has, since 1972, become the world's largest grain importer.

In sum, under the best management, Soviet farmers could not produce yields comparable to those achieved in Western Europe and the United States where the climate is more favorable for agriculture.

On the positive side, The USSR is a vast storehouse of fossil fuels and minerals. Within its boundaries are large deposits of many scarce, often strategic, minerals. The Soviet Union, not Saudi Arabia, is the world's largest oil producer. Moreover, it has vast deposits of natural gas. Thus, in this age of growing interdependence among nations, the USSR has become a major exporter of such resources, especially to Eastern and Western Europe. Moreover, the export of energy (both oil and natural gas), gold, timber, and several minerals has become the principal source of the hard currency badly needed for the increased import of technology and food. (The authorities strictly prohibit the export of the ruble; thus it is not a convertible currency.)

The vastness of the country, the seemingly unending steppes, and the bountiful natural resources have been major factors contributing to the attitude of gigantomania (gigantism) that often dominates Soviet thinking. This is a Russian feeling of expansiveness that seems to arise out of an awe for the vast reaches of Russian land. It now probably incorporates the communist tendency to regard large industrial and agricultural enterprises as inherently superior to smaller enterprises. What is big is good; what is bigger is better; what is biggest is best!

However, the hugeness of the USSR is a mixed blessing.

By nearly any standard of measure, surface transport is woefully inadequate. The rail network is thin and there is nothing comparable to the four-lane highway systems of Western Europe and the United States. In the rural areas the inadequate communications infrastructure is a major problem. Rural hard-surfaced roads are very rare. Thus, many, perhaps most, of the roads to collective and state farms are snowed or mudded in many days each year.

River transport is important, but nearly all the navigable rivers run north and south, whereas the main traffic is east and west. With the major exception of the Black Sea outlet to the Mediterranean Sea, most Soviet seaports are frozen for several months each year.

The Historical and Human Influences

The geographic factors and forces that shaped tsarist affairs, and that now affect Soviet affairs, are inexorably linked with history.

Significantly influenced by such factors as the location of the best agricultural land in the western regions and the harsh climate of Siberia, the bulk of the population is concentrated in the Baltic republics, the Ukraine, and the western region of the Russian Republic (RSFSR). Slightly over half of the population is ethnic Russian, most of whom live in the Russian Republic. As of the late 1980s, however, the Muslim people of Central Asia are the fastest-growing population, with projections that they will pass the Russians in number during the next century. Altogether there are some 100 different ethnic groups that speak scores of different languages.

The absence of mountain or water barriers between the country and its two most important continental neighbors has been a major factor in tsarist and Soviet history. Using the Polish plain as a land bridge, the French army under Napoléon (early in the 1800s) and German armies (twice in this century) found the road to Russia easy to travel. The Polish plain of invasion is a major reason why Poland is the Soviet Union's most important client state, serving as a buffer to aggression from the west. Similarly, in the east the vast level steppes of Siberia provide no natural impediment to an adventurous invader. In about 1223 the Tatars swept in from the east, penetrated as far west as Germany, and maintained sovereignty over Russia for some 250 years. Thus, Napoléon's famed remark: "Scratch a Russian and you will find a Tatar." Suspicion of foreigners is a universal trait. Understandably, given their history, the Soviet people, especially the Russians, suffer an acute case of xenophobia.

There is no room in these pages to recount the fluctuating liberal and reactionary behavior of the various autocrats that have ruled both the tsarist and the Soviet empires. However, note must be made that the system of rule always has been authoritarian. As Nobel laureate Alexander Solzhenitsyn has stressed, authoritarianism is an ingrained part of the Russian political culture. Thus, he believes that if the Marxist-Leninist dictatorship were to crumble, the only viable alternative to the present system would be a new form of religious authoritarian rule. The Russian Orthodox church was a mainstay of tsarist authoritarian control.

Many observers believe that a political culture nurtured under a thousand years of unbroken authoritarian rule provided fertile ground for the Marxist-Leninist dictatorship. Studies of the values and attitudes of emigrants from the Soviet Union reveal important beliefs that fit more with authoritarian than democratic political culture. For example, large numbers of the émigrés are frightened to learn that in the West an individual must find his or her own job. The state should provide employment for its citizens.

The tsarist experience, which incorporated a state bureaucracy, the nobles, and the church, taught that there was security in strong leaders who provided the right answers to the problems of life. Although claiming a different base, the Soviet system provides strong leaders and claims it has the right guidelines for all human affairs. As discussed in the section, "Shared Values and Beliefs," Marxism-Leninism is said to be "the science of society" that provides the basis for correct human behavior in all areas of life.

Closely related to this experience, there was a strong sense of messianism under tsardom, especially among the majority who adhered to the Russian Orthodox faith. Surely that conviction helped pave the way for the acceptance of a new faith that the world will achieve the nirvana of communism, led by Moscow.

The vast majority of the population in 1917 was peasant and, as compared to much of Western Europe and North America, their experience was not that of free individualistic farmers.

Serfdom was ended in 1861, but the village commune (that is, the individual village society) and the mir (the council) remained strong. Led by the village elder (starosta), each male head of a household (dvor) sat on a council that dominated village life. No aspect of life was immune from the council's hand, for it could and did undertake periodic redistribution of the land, determine times for sowing and harvesting, and even resolve problems that arose between husbands and wives.

Even though there was widespread peasant resistance to Stalin's "revolution from above" that forced the rural population into the collective and state farms in the 1930s, there was much about the new farms that was familiar to Russian historical experience. Indeed, the kolkhoz (collective farm) of the 1930s was based on the old village.

Private ownership by the masses and, especially, individual entrepreneurship, had weak roots in tsarist society.

Although the Duma (a quasi-representative, parliamentary institution) came into being after the 1905 revolt, it was never allowed to flower fully. Political parties were outlawed. Thus, the political parties that sprang up around the turn of the century not only were illegal, but much of their activity was secret.

Some otherwise astute observers of Russia in the early years of the century, such as the British journalist Sir Donald Mackenzie Wallace, thought that Russia was destined to evolve into a modern democratic state, guided by a benevolent monarchy, as had occurred in Great Britain. However, not only did the tsarist system continue to crumble under its own corruption, but what might have been was shattered by the devastating defeat at the hands of the German armies in World War I. The last tsar, Nicholas II, abdicated, and the weak Provisional Government lasted for only part of 1917.

In October (Julian calendar; November by the Gregorian calendar) 1917, led by Vladimir I. Lenin, the Bolsheviks staged a successful coup d'état that marked the beginning of a revolution. That beginning included the 1918–21 **Civil War** fought between the Bolshevik Red Army and the White Army, the latter supported in part by interventionist forces, including British and U.S. expeditionary troops.

Although the Red Army was victorious, Lenin and his followers were far from agreement over the future course of the new system, including even whether or not there was to be a state at all.

Lenin was the founding father of Bolshevik rule, but he fell ill in 1921 and, never fully recovering, died in 1924. Thus, the politics of the early years were dominated by the struggle for Lenin's mantle, with the primary contenders being Stalin and Trotsky.

The points at issue were often complex, but central to the debate that ensued was whether effort should be concentrated upon building a Soviet state system, eventually Stalin's major stress, or whether Trotsky's push for using the Bolshevik Russian base as the headquarters for conducting a "permanent [worldwide] revolution" was to receive top priority.

Much of Trotsky's thinking was rooted in the iskra (spark) theory. Essentially, the thought was that war-ravaged, industrialized Western Europe was ripe for a communist revolution. Thus, the fortuitous communist base established in Russia would provide the necessary spark to ignite a real Marxist revolution in Western Europe. Once communism was firmly established in most advanced Europe, it would help backward Russia and the rest of the world into the initial stages of building world communism.

From the beginning, Stalin won the major battles. Trotsky was exiled in 1926 and, after Stalin had captured the countryside by imposing the collective and state farms on the peasants in the early 1930s, the so-called Stalin Constitution was promulgated in 1936, accompanied by the now open claim that "socialism in one country" was being built.

The House That Stalin Built

Much change has occurred in the Soviet Union since Stalin's death in March 1953. If the "restructuring" (perestroika) that Gorbachev is attempting to carry out is achieved, the changes made during an extended Gorbachev era will be greater than any changes since the institution of the Soviet system under Lenin and Stalin. However, at this writing, the Soviet social, economic, and political system remains essentially that which was imposed upon the nation between 1917 and 1953.

There are many similarities between the Soviet system and systems more familiar to the reader, such as that of the United States. However, the differences are so important that they call for the knowledge of a special lexicon of terms and concepts such as the one produced here. With emphasis on the differences, some important characteristics of the Soviet system are these:

All of the land is owned by the state.

Virtually all economic enterprise is owned and directed by the state.

With the exception of the children and the elderly, virtually every citizen works in the USSR, Inc.

With the exception of private plot produce sold in the collective farm markets (kolkhoz markets) and a few private service activities, there are virtually no legal private enterprises, no markets, and no prices that fluctuate according to supply and demand. Nearly the entire economy is controlled by state plans.

In spite of the call for "openness" (glasnost) there is no legal private press, because all publishing and broadcasting is monopolized by party and state institutions. Only that sanctioned by party and state officials is fit to print or broadcast.

The party jealously guards its claim to having a monopoly over leadership and decision making on all matters that it deems important—that is, "the right to control" (pravo kontrolia). Even under the Gorbachev reforms, where more than one candidate has been offered for elected posts at some local levels, the nominees undoubtedly have had to pass party approval.

The ultimate measure of the rightness or justice of any activity is the so-called "science of society" (that is, Marxism-Leninism) which is said to govern all human activity.

The ultimate directorate of all activity, including the final interpretation of the laws of the "science of society" is the party, with the Politburo having the final say in all matters.

In the USSR "the collective" is stressed and the individual is downplayed.

In sum, the USSR is the world's most bureaucratized society within which, as Khrushchev said, "we the leaders are responsible for everything." Guided by central planning and direction in all realms, the USSR, Inc., is not just a command economy, it is a command society.

Four major components of any viable socioeconomic-political system are (1) shared values and beliefs, largely the stuff of nationalism; (2) political institutions and practices; (3) economic institutions and practices; and (4) society and its social and political culture. The particular nature of any system is largely a reflection of the interaction of these components.

Shared Values and Beliefs: The New Soviet Nationalism

As Robert McIver observed in his classic work *The Web of Government,* a crucial base of any society is its "myth-system." The "myth-system" is the "value-impregnated beliefs and notions that men hold, that they live by or live for. Every society is held together by a myth-system, a complex of dominating thought-forms that determines and sustains all its activities. . . . Every civilization, every period, every nation has its characteristic myth-complex. In it lies the secret of social unities and social continuities, and its changes compose the inner history of every society."[1]

Not only did Stalin preside over building and shaping most of the institutions that dominate the Soviet scene, but his rule served to influence profoundly the beliefs and values that guide the leaders and the people.

In a section below, "Political Socialization and Political Culture," we discuss in some detail how the attitudes and behavior of the mass of Soviet society are influenced to reflect the official body of values and beliefs that the leadership continually espouses. A major, unending debate among outside observers of the Soviet Union centers upon the question of just what the Soviet people and their leaders really believe. There is little disagreement, however, over two important universal influences.

First, nationalism is the essential emotional cement that holds all modern nation-states together. Without a minimal level of nationalism, made up largely of shared beliefs and values, nations are in serious trouble. Major discord can lead to civil war and revolution. True, there is evidence of discord in the USSR. Dissent is important. Nevertheless, as compared with that of many other nations, the level of civil disruption and disobedience in the Soviet Union has been held to a minimum in recent decades.

Second, legitimization is an essential ingredient of any viable system. Marxism-Leninism (especially the doctrines of Lenin) is infiltrated by lingering strains of traditional Russian nationalism; it is the lingua franca of Soviet political discourse; it also provides the ultimate justification for the policies and deeds of the party leaders. Stalin deified Lenin, claiming that the corpus of his writings provided a "science of society." Subsequently, every leader in every major speech has pointed to the discoveries of Lenin as the unassailable justification for his actions and proposals.

In 1936 Stalin found appropriate passages in Lenin's writings to bolster his claim that under his leadership "socialism in one country" was being constructed. In his 1956 de-Stalinization speech, Khrushchev invoked Lenin's observations to support his condemnation of Stalin's abuse of power. Brezhnev proclaimed that following the path charted by Lenin, the USSR had reached the advanced stage of "developed socialism." Gorbachev justifies his call for "restructuring" as a need to return to the true Leninist model.

The tsars had secret police. Lenin created the Cheka—the first Soviet secret police. Stalin went further: he legitimized mass terror as a key element of Soviet rule. Since Stalin, mass terror, in terms of the incarceration of millions charged with political subversion, has been discontinued. However, secret police still exist (the KGB), and the belief remains that criticism of the Soviet state is traitorous and is punishable by law.

The Soviet Union is a dictatorship led by an oligarchy centered on the Politburo. Central to the working of the system is the Leninist doctrine of "democratic centralism." Assertedly, there is free discussion and deliberation of all issues by the party and the public until a decision is made. However, once the decision is made, it becomes law and every member must follow it. Not only is no further discussion tolerated, but because the party always insists upon setting the agenda, central control—not grass-roots democracy—is the ruling principle.

Still, the central question remains: what do the Soviet people believe? Yes, dissent exists, particularly among the ethnic and religious minorities. Yet, even with their private doubts, most of the Soviet people seem to regard themselves as good Soviet citizens. Even beyond the relative calm that pervades the society, perhaps the most important single piece of evidence that most of the citizenry accepts the basic system can be found in the realm of political dissent. First of all, the expression of public political dissent is far less common than religious and national dissent. Second, where political dissent has surfaced, overwhelmingly it has been communist in content. Thus, the call has been less to change the system than it has been a cry that the current leaders are not acting as proper Marxist-Leninists.

Party and State Institutions: The Party Monopoly of Rule

If asked to describe the essence of the Soviet political system in a few words, one is tempted to reply that, dominated by the Politburo, the Communist Party of the Soviet Union runs everything. In a sense that is true. The leaders do try to be "responsible for everything." However, the Soviet system is complex. Although the party jealously guards its monopoly over all key leadership positions, the governmental institutions and society also are important.

There is only one party. No other parties are allowed. Moreover, factionalism within the party is illegal. However, less than 10 percent of the population belongs to the party. It is the elite "vanguard of society," originally fashioned by Lenin. Although, with some exceptions, application for membership is open to all adult Soviet citizens, screening processes, including a period of candidate membership, are designed to keep the party a select minority devoted to championing the party cause. The primary party cause is the perpetuation of its members' monopoly over power. Individuals who are excluded from membership include those with criminal records, those who openly profess a religious faith, and those who do not demonstrate the proper commitment to and discipline for the party cause.

Paralleling the government bureaucratic hierarchy at all levels, the party hierarchy extends from the primary party groups (the party cells of an earlier era) on the farms and in the factories and other local institutions to the Politburo in Moscow. At each administrative level (that is, in the farm or factory, the district or city, and at the regional, republic, and national levels) there is a party executive committee led by a party secretary.

Because the Moscow-based Politburo is the ruling executive committee of the several-hundred-member Central Committee of the Communist Party of the Soviet Union (CC CPSU) that seldom meets, the Politburo is the center of Soviet political power.

Even though the Central Committee is not normally an important deliberative body, membership on it is important. Aside from a tiny handful of token peasants and ordinary workers, who usually serve for only one term between the party congresses (which meet only every five years), the great bulk of the members of the Politburo and the Secretariat) belong because they hold important posts in the party or state apparatuses. The heads of the key national ministries, the party secretaries of each of the fourteen constituent republics other than the RSFSR (the general secretary also serves as the secretary for the Russian Republic), and the party secretaries of key administrative regions are also members of the Central Committee. New members of the Politburo and the Secretariat always serve an apprentice period on the Central Committee.

The party committees in the administrative hierarchy below Moscow are highly active and are responsible for all political affairs on the level at which they are formed and for supervising the party activities of the units below that level. For example, at the region (oblast or krai) administration level—areas roughly the size of small U.S. states—there are obkoms (or kraikoms), party executive committees responsible for all political activities within the region, including monitoring the activities of the district (raion) or city (gorod) party committees (raikoms or gorkoms) in that region. Most raions are roughly the size of U.S. counties. Moreover, because the party enjoys a leadership over all affairs, an obkom is held responsible also for the oblast soviet (state) committee's (oblispolkom) activities and, indeed, for all affairs within the region.

At the peak of the pyramid of power is the first (or general) secretary of the CPSU (Khrushchev, Brezhnev, or Gorbachev) who is the chairman of the Politburo and, therefore, the supreme leader of the party and the nation.

Alongside the Politburo is the Secretariat, which is primarily charged with overseeing the fulfillment of party policy. Key Soviet party leaders, including the general secretary, serve in both the Politburo and the Secretariat.

According to party rules, lower party bodies elect higher party officials, including the delegates to the party congresses, which usually meet only every five years but, theoretically, constitute the ultimate source of power for the Central Committee and its executive committee, the Politburo. In practice, however, all nominees for all important posts are selected by higher party officials from the nomenklatura, which is the heart of the Soviet patron-client system.

At all levels of both the party and state hierarchies, the nomenklatura system is of crucial importance. Generated by party authorities at each level in the hierarchy, the nomenklatura is an appointments list containing the names of individuals approved as suitable for appointment to all important party and state posts for which the party group is responsible. For example, an individual nominated for election as chairman of a collective farm is, in fact, someone approved by the oblast party committee. Similarly, although new members of the Politburo are theoretically elected by the Central Committee, in practice, the new members of that most powerful political body are co-opted by the standing Politburo members.

Given the party monopoly over power and leadership and the nomenklatura system, party membership, loyal service to the party, and success in one's work assignments are not all that is needed to assure advancement for an ambitious

Soviet individual. Equally important for the ambitious party member is faithful service to a party superior who is his or her patron. Thus, the formulation of patron-client relations is as important for a successful Soviet politician as is the ability to attract voter support for a successful U.S. politician.

On the government side of the Soviet system of rule, party membership and successful party activity are virtually as important for someone who is a governmental official as they are for someone whose career is totally within the party hierarchy. In recent decades all of the directors of factories and the collective farm chairmen also have been party members, as are all the key administrators of higher state posts. Indeed, with relatively rare exceptions, those who rise to high positions in the Soviet Union have a career of to-and-froing between party and state posts. For example, a party member's first important position might be either in a local party or state office, followed by an upward climb, serving for a time as a key raion government official, later as an oblast party secretary, and finally winding up as a minister heading a national governmental office.

In name, the Soviet governmental system is federal. Reading the Constitution could lead one to conclude that considerable powers are reserved for the fifteen constituent republics. In practice, however, the Soviet governmental system is unitary. Of course, Moscow cannot possibly manage everything. Therefore, lower state officials often exercise some initiative. However, if Moscow decides to intervene in any matter, anywhere, it always has the last word.

On paper, the elected Supreme Soviet is the focal point of governmental power and authority. However, its several hundred members meet only for a few weeks a year, when their primary task is to ratify (always unanimously) legislative action already in place.

The heads of the ministeries (for example, foreign affairs or agriculture) and the members of the Presidium of the Supreme Soviet are all "elected" members of the Supreme Soviet. However, their real power derives from the high offices that they hold in the bureaucracy.

The more important ministers constitute the Council of Ministers charged with coordinating day-to-day governmental affairs. The chairman of the Council of Ministers is a rough counterpart of a Western European prime minister.

The Presidium of the Supreme Soviet is an executive committee of the Supreme Soviet serving primarily as the chief legislative body between sessions of the Supreme Soviet. It also exercises some judicial responsibilities such as interpreting laws. The chairman of the Presidium of the Supreme Soviet is a rough counterpart of a Western president and serves as the head of state.

Western observers often refer to the "troika" (team of three), when "collective leadership" (as contrasted with Stalin's "cult of personality") is being stressed. The troika consists of the chairman of the Council of Ministers, the chairman of the Presidium of the Supreme Soviet, and the general secretary of the CPSU. Again, however, even though he may hold no high state office, the general secretary is the most powerful individual. Moreover, the real source of power of the chairman of the Council of Ministers and the chairman of the Presidium of the Supreme Soviet is the fact that such individuals are also key members of the Politburo.

In the judicial realm, there is a hierarchy of state prosecutors and courts. At the pinnacle are the Moscow-based Supreme Court and the Procurator General. The latter serves as the attorney general for the USSR. The Supreme Court is the highest court in the land but, unlike in the United States, it does not have the power of judicial review. Thus, the final interpreter of law is the party—ultimately, the Politburo.

Built into the hand-in-glove party–state system of controls is a problem-causing contradiction that has plagued the Soviet system of rule from the beginning.

Strictly according to the rules, local state officials are directly responsible for day-to-day social and governmental affairs, such as making production-related decisions in the factories and on the farms. Direct activity in such realms is not the responsibility of regional and local party officials. Nevertheless, especially since Stalin's time, the leaders from

Khrushchev to Gorbachev have repeatedly complained about overzealous regional and local party officials intruding into production decision making.

In the USSR where the leaders are "responsible for everything," everything is political. Therefore, for example, if things are not going well in a local area, and the farms are not meeting state-mandated grain deliveries to state collection points, it is the local party officials who receive the threatening telegrams and phone calls from higher party authorities.

When local scandals arise or plans are not met, local party officials' careers are on the line. Just as the general secretary is the most powerful person in the USSR, at the regional and district level, the party prefects—that is, the oblast and raion party secretaries—are the most powerful individuals at that level of the interlocked party–state hierarchies.

Economic Institutions and Practices: A State Monopoly

Because virtually every enterprise is owned and operated by the Soviet state, the primary business of government in the USSR is the direction and management of economic affairs.

As dictated by Marxist-Leninist doctrine, free markets and free prices are outlawed capitalist evils. Therefore, it is the duty of higher authorities to decide what will be produced in what quality and quantity and sold at what price. Assertedly, taxes are minimal in the USSR. By some measures that is correct. In practice, however, the Soviet people may be the most highly taxed citizens in the world.

The great bulk of the state revenue collected by Moscow is in the form of a turnover tax. As nearly everything sold in the USSR is sold by the state, and all prices are arbitrarily set by central bureaucrats, the single largest source of state funds comes from the sale of items (for example, vodka, automobiles, fur coats, and other luxuries) that are priced far above the cost of production.

All important economic decisions are dictated by the

Moscow-based party–state bureaucracy. On the state side of the equation, one of the most important government organs is the central state planning agency Gosplan.

Every factory, farm, or enterprise (including the newspapers and schools) is tied to Gosplan and its responsibility for planning all activity. The five-year plans provide long-term goals that are broken down into yearly and monthly targets, not only for the nation but also for each enterprise. The twelfth five-year plan is for the years 1986–90. For example, in some office in Moscow is a plan that designates how many university students studying to be English language teachers will be graduated in the year 1990.

Unfortunately, practice has shown that events that cannot be foreseen often play havoc with the best-laid Moscow plans. Fires, floods, and human failures often mean that, for example, the materials needed for a particular construction project are not available at the time needed. Therefore, throughout the economy, the illegal practice of blat along with the tolkach have been winked at as essential ingredients necessary to make the system work.

Blat is pull, contacts, or influence to assure that plan targets will be achieved when the prescribed system has broken down. For example, if a construction project has been brought to a halt because the planned nails have not been delivered, blat will be used to obtain them from some other enterprise that has an excess of nails: hoarding of scarce materials is widespread in the USSR. In the deal, a case of vodka, scarce theater tickets, or the promise of returning the favor at some future time are usually involved.

The tolkach is the expediter. Usually the tolkach is someone on the payroll of the enterprise, say an engineer, whose primary purpose is to cut red tape and do what is necessary to assure that the enterprise in question fulfills its commitments according to plan. Again, plan is the key, especially as related to bonuses.

Lacking a marketplace and free prices, but with state enterprises that are not allowed to go broke and with guaranteed minimum wages, profit is of little importance to Soviet enterprise directors and their workers. What is most important is meeting plan, because bonuses and promotions are tied primarily to that achievement.

For the vast majority of Soviet workers, just earning the guaranteed minimum wage does not provide a comfortable living Soviet style. Thus, to do well, workers know that their enterprises need to overfulfill plan, but not by too much. Overfulfilling plan in just the right amount may assure a relatively decent income this year, but overfulfilling it by too much carries the threat of the state's raising the plan target and thus making next year's achievement more difficult.

The need to meet plan and, if possible, slightly exceed it, is a prime motivating factor for blat and the tolkach. It also is the root of the practice of "storming." Often a plant and its workers approach the end of a plan period, such as a month, and discover that they are behind schedule. As a result, furtive efforts, including working overtime, are made to assure that they will not be penalized for failure to meet the plan. This is called "storming."

Largely outside of direct central control are the tiny peasant private plots, occupying some 3 percent of the sown area, and the very small private service sector. The bulk of such enterprise is conducted during off hours by peasants and state employees who are full-time workers in the factories, farms, and offices, because nearly every able-bodied adult is expected to work full time for the USSR, Inc.

Theoretically, as contrasted with the workers on the sovkhozy (state-owned and -operated farms) who receive a state guaranteed minimum salary, the workers on the kolkhozy (collective farms) are members of cooperatives, whose output determines their incomes. However, with changes initiated by Khrushchev, including a minimum income for the kolkhoz workers (guaranteed by a state-mandated crop insurance program) and, especially, the installation of party controls within all of the farms, today there is essentially little difference between the sovkhozy and the kolkhozy. Again, therefore, the great bulk of the adult citizenry are plugged into the all-encompassing party–state bureaucratic hierarchy at some level, with the ordinary factory worker, office worker, and peasant at the bottom rung of the ladder.

Every local enterprise, be it a school or factory, is at the bottom of a pyramid of controls that extends from the national or republic level downward. Thus, everything from the production mix in a factory to the funds allocated for wages is subject to central direction.

Wage differentials are not as high in the USSR as they are in other countries. However, the income of an important manager is much higher than that of an ordinary worker. Moreover, when the extra perquisites received by high officials are accounted for (the use of a state-owned car; a chauffeur; state-paid expenses; a country dacha, or vacation home; and access to special shops), those highly placed in the USSR are very much better off than most workers.

Political Socialization and Political Culture

As described by political scientists, political culture is the collection of political attitudes, beliefs, and values shared by most citizens. Political socialization is the process by which the citizens in a society, from childhood on, arrive at their shared attitudes, beliefs, and values.

One of the most important aspects of Soviet society is rooted in the hard-to-translate concept of the obshchina—roughly "the collective."

As noted earlier, in predominantly peasant tsarist Russia, the village commune and the mir fostered collective activity and responsibility while downplaying the individual. The attitudes engendered by that experience fit nicely with the doctrines of Marxism-Leninism and the goal of creating the ideal "new Soviet man." According to the ideal, such a person is totally unselfish, marked by a Marxist-Leninist social consciousness, and thus totally devoted to "the collective."

At the local level, every individual in the schools, economic enterprises, and so on is identified as a member of a collective. Nationwide, all citizens are said to be part of the larger Soviet collective. Collective identification is not passive; it is actively fostered.

For example, in the primary schools the children in a class are divided in zvenya—small links or teams. Rewards and punishments are directed largely at the links rather than at the individual. Similarly, activity is organized in the factories and on the farms, and "collective competitions" are instituted among such groups.

In party, union, and farm meetings, kritika i samokritika (criticism and self-criticism) are important tools of political socialization. For example, if an erring worker has been late, drunk on the job, or whatever, he or she is expected to stand up before a meeting of peers, confess these sins and promise to do better. Moreover, he or she is expected to report on similar transgressions committed by colleagues.

The party–state monopoly over the press and broadcast media is a powerful tool for shaping public attitudes and beliefs. Former Soviet journalists report that although censors exist, their need to delete material is relatively rare. Such institutions as the Writer's Union train Soviet journalists to be their own censors. Writers and broadcasters hold privileged positions, and membership in the unions is essential to the pursuit of their careers. Expulsion from the union is a major punishment used against those who break the rules.

Some Soviet citizens listen to foreign broadcasts beamed to the USSR, when they are not being jammed. Listening is not illegal, but reporting the falsehoods heard (especially if the material is critical of the USSR) is a crime that often results in serious punishment.

Dissenters with a literary bent produce illegal samizdat (literally, self-edited) tracts, which are often copied by their sympathizers. However, those who produce such material that is judged to be seriously threatening to the system are often caught and punished, sometimes by long imprisonment.

Though dissent does exist, Soviet society is marked by correct overt public behavior. Anyone who has traveled on the Moscow subway can tell you that it is freer of litter and graffiti than most U.S. university buildings. Moreover, if some wayward individual does drop a cigarette butt on the subway floor, there is considerable likelihood that a babushka (grandmother or old woman), rather than a uniformed guard, will accost the sinner and deliver a lecture on this errant behavior.

Virtually every eligible worker belongs to the centrally directed labor unions. Strikes are illegal and the unions do not negotiate for higher wages, but everyone belongs because the unions do play an important role in matters such as managing pensions and obtaining scarce housing, and because joining is the thing to do.

From Lenin onward, the leadership has continually referred to the collective farms and unions as "schools of communism." Their primary function is to promote correct collective behavior. Union and farm meetings include lectures by party propagandists explaining the latest line out of Moscow—for example, the importance of "openness" and "restructuring" to improving the economy. The most important local union committee is the "production committee" in which the workers are encouraged to contribute ideas that will enhance achieving plan targets.

Soviet elections are not important in the sense that those elected to party and state offices necessarily have a popular mandate to fulfill. Yet, the turnout for elections generally exceeds 99 percent of the eligible voters. Why? Election day has been transformed into a national celebration of the achievements of Soviet society, and voting is an important thing to be done by all the members of the national collective.

Most people in most societies do not judge their position by external standards. What is important to them is how they fare in comparison to their grandparents, parents, and peers. For most Americans Soviet life would be drab, unrewarding, and restricting. However, for most Soviet citizens, life has improved, especially since Stalin's time, and they are as well off as most of their neighbors. This has an important positive impact on their view of the system.

In our view, the creation of the ideal "new Soviet man" does not square with human nature. Nevertheless, for reasons suggested here, political socialization as practiced in the USSR has gone a long way toward shaping overt public behavior in ways desired by the leaders.

Conclusion: Avoiding Mirror-imaging

The world over, people put on their trousers one leg at a time. All human beings hurt and bleed when cut. Yet, as already stressed above, important differences do exist among societies.

Human beings everywhere tend to view the world and other societies through the familiar lenses of their own experiences. Such mirror-imaging is natural, but it is responsible for much of the misunderstanding that exists in the world, including Western misconceptions about the Soviet system.

Our major advice to anyone who is beginning for the first time to study the USSR is to try to set aside preconceptions based upon his or her experiences and knowledge about his or her own system.

Elections as practiced in the Soviet Union are not the same as Western elections. Soviet labor unions play a significantly different role than do unions in most nations. Much else that is familiar in the West is different in the USSR. Indeed, "truth" as seen through Soviet eyes, at least as it is officially defined, is also quite different.

What is true in the USSR, as repeatedly stated by Soviet philosophers, is rooted in the Marxist-Leninist "science of society" that is said to provide the base for all correct attitudes and behavior. Therefore, individual and collective success and progress can come only from activities determined by the "perception of necessity." This is to say that the only correct Soviet way is to know and practice the "laws" discovered by Marx and Lenin, especially as interpreted by the current party leadership.

Note

1. R. M. McIver, *The Web of Government,* The Macmillan Company, New York, 1948, pp. 4 and 5.

Selected Monographs

Barry, Donald D., and Barry, Carol Barner. *Contemporary Soviet Politics: An Introduction.* Englewood Cliffs, N.J.: Prentice-Hall Inc., 1987.

Bialer, Seweryn. *Stalin's Successors: Leadership Stability and Change in the Soviet Union.* New York: Cambridge University Press, 1980.

Fletcher, William C. *Soviet Believers: The Religious Sector of the Population.* Lawrence, Kans.: The Regents Press of Kansas, 1981.

Goldman, Marshall I. *USSR in Crisis: The Failure of an Economic System.* New York: W. W. Norton, 1983.

Hammer, Darrell P. *The USSR: The Politics of Oligarchy.* Boulder, Colo.: Westview, 1986.

Hill, Ronald J., and Frank, Peter. *The Soviet Communist Party.* London: Allen & Unwin, 1986.

Kerblay, Basile. *Modern Soviet Society.* New York: Pantheon Books, 1983.

Kort, Michael. *The Soviet Colossus: A History of the USSR.* New York: Charles Scribner's Sons, 1985.

Laird, Roy D. *The Politburo: Demographic Trends, Gorbachev, and the Future.* Boulder, Colo.: Westview, 1986.

Lydolph, Paul E. *Geography of the USSR.* Elkhart Lake, Wis.: Misty Valley Publishing, 1979.

Nove, Alec. *Socialism, Economics and Development.* London: Allen & Unwin, 1986.

Rubenstein, Alvin Z. *Soviet Foreign Policy since World War II: Imperial and Global.* Boston: Little, Brown, 1985.

The Lexicon

Note: In the definitions, **boldface** type indicates a word that is defined elsewhere in the *Lexicon*. *Italic* type indicates a synonym without its own entry in the *Lexicon*. Russian equivalents are given after the main entry in roman type, in parentheses.

able-bodied workers Full-time workers. Especially applicable to full-time farm workers to distinguish them from their dependents, who also live on the farms but devote, at most, only part of their time to work on the farms.

Academician (akademik) A member of one of the national or republic academies of sciences.

Academy of Sciences (Akademia nauk) The highly prestigious scholarly body whose membership represents a wide range of scholarly endeavors. Only the most distinguished Soviet scientists and scholars are members.

active (aktiv) The most active members of the party organization. Also nonparty members who actively pursue state and party causes. See **nonparty active.**

adjuncts A western term used to describe collectively the various Soviet institutions, outside the employment setting, that are designed to inculcate into the citizens proper Soviet attitudes and behavior—for example, the young organizations, comrades' courts, and the like.

advanced farms The small percentage of collective and state farms that are markedly superior economically to the great bulk of Soviet farms.

advanced socialism A level of Soviet development. Rejecting Khrushchev's claim in the early 1960s that the

USSR had achieved the initial stage of communism, Brezhnev and his successors have asserted that the present stage of Soviet development is "advanced socialism," implying a stage of development that is just prior to the entry into communism. Also called *developed socialism.*

advokat A Soviet lawyer.

Aeroflot The Soviet state airline.

agitation Party activity designed to shape mass attitudes and behavior along desired lines.

agitator Dispenser of political information to the public and collector of political intelligence for the party. A propaganda agent who senses public mood and concern and conveys this vital information to the leadership.

agitprop (Otdel agitatsii i propagandy) The propaganda department. The agitation and propaganda section of the Central Committee Secretariat. It has the general responsibility for mass agitation and party propaganda throughout Soviet society. See **propaganda.**

agitpunkt Agitation center. A local office that dispenses official propaganda and information to the citizens.

agricultural artel Rural cooperative. Especially in the early years, the collective farms were sometimes referred to as agricultural artels.

agrogorod Agricultural city. In 1949 Khrushchev advocated a scheme, never consumated, that would have transformed the amalgamated state and collective farms into rural cities.

agro-industrial complex (agro-promyshlennyi kompleks) The APK. The aggregate of farms and agriculturally related industrial enterprises in an area.

agro-industrial district union (raionnaia promyshlennaia organizatsiia) The rapo or raion industrial organization. Unified management of farms and agriculturally related industrial enterprises within a district.

akademgorodok The Siberian Division of the USSR Academy of Sciences.

akademik See **academician.**

aktiv See **active.**

alienation, theory of A Marxist doctrine stating that the exploited workers under capitalism are alienated from their work and from society.

allied intervention Participation by several Western allied powers in the 1918–21 Russian Civil War. When the Bolsheviks withdrew from the war with Germany in 1918, several Western powers (including France, Great Britain, and the United States) sent expeditionary forces into Russia to aid the White Army in its struggle against the Bolshevik Red Army.

"all power to the soviets" Bolshevik slogan in 1917 calling for an end to "dual power" through the overthrow of the Provisional Government and the creation of a truly revolutionary order based upon soviets. Bolsheviks took up the slogan after Lenin's return to Russia in April 1917, even though they were still a minority in the soviets.

All-Union Central Council of Trade Unions The central controlling unit of all industrial unions.

All-Union Farm Machinery Association An organization formed in 1961, replacing the MTS (machine tractor stations) and RTS (repair and technical service stations). The organization is in charge of farm machinery, fertilizer sales, and spare parts for machinery repair.

all-union ministries Supreme Soviet ministries that do not have counterpart ministries at the republic level.

amalgamations Starting in 1952, on Khrushchev's initiative, neighboring collective and state farms were joined to create the present huge kolkhozy and sovkhozy.

Antarctic Treaty A 1959 U.S.–Soviet agreement prohibiting the militarization of the Antarctic continent.

antiparasite laws Legislative enactments that define and outlaw specific social and economic actions as nonproductive and that designate those who practice them as "parasites." An example of a parasite would be an able-bodied Soviet adult who lives off black market activities and is not officially employed.

antiparty group Members of the CPSU Presidium (Politburo) who unsuccessfully attempted to oust Khrushchev as first secretary in 1957.

APK See **agro-industrial complex.**

apparat An administrative organization or bureaucracy, such as the trade union apparat or the apparat of a ministry. Without a qualifier, the term refers to the apparat of the party.

apparatchik Members of the apparatus. The practical workers of the party or government organization, the people who often worked up through the ranks from a lowly origin. They are to be differentiated from the intellectuals, or the "old leaders." Sometimes the term is used in a derogatory sense.

April Theses A proclamation of intent made by Lenin upon his return to Petrograd in April 1971. The theses advocated "all power to the soviets"; seizure of the landed estates; refusal to cooperate with the Provisional Government; and a complete break of the Bolsheviks from the Mensheviks.

artel A producers' cooperative. Originally applied to industrial cooperatives among itinerant workers but later expanded to include collective farms and artisans' groups. See **collective farm.**

aspirant A degree-seeking graduate student or assistant.

assessors Citizens elected to sit in court with the judges and decide both criminal and civil cases. Two of these untrained individuals and one judge hear each case in the people's courts, and then hand down a majority decision.

ASSR See **autonomous republic.**

atheism Disbelief in the existence of a deity. In the Soviet Union, atheism, based upon the "scientific" teachings of Marxism-Leninism, is advocated officially. It is taught as a required course in all Soviet higher educational institutions, along with propaganda against religion as superstition and prejudice. All religious believers are excluded from the party, although party members sometimes attend religious funerals, weddings, and other church functions.

attestat A high school diploma or a recommendation.

authoritarianism A political system in which an individual or a group of individuals (that is, an oligarchy) has a monopoly over political and economic power and decision making.

autocracy (samoderzhavie) The authoritarian political order under the tsarist regimes in which all sovereign power was in the hands of the tsar.

autonomous oblast A large region created to represent a minority nationality. Each one sends five deputies to the Supreme Soviet.

autonomous republic An ASSR. A territorial division. There are twenty Autonomous Soviet Social Republics (most of which are in the Russian Republic) created to recognize large national minorities not given full republic status. Subordinate to republic authority, they do administer some governmental affairs and are represented by deputies in the Soviet of Nationalities.

Autonomous Soviet Socialist Republics The ASSR. See **autonomous republic.**

autonomous territories The okrug. A small geographic area (all ten are in the RSFSR) created in recognition of small national groups that are represented in the Soviet of Nationalities, each by one deputy.

babushka A grandmother, or any old woman.

Baikal-Amur Mainline The BAM. A new rail line across Eastern Siberia and the Soviet Far East, located two to three hundred kilometers north of the Trans-Siberian Railroad.

BAM See **Baikal-Amur Mainline.**

Barbarossa The code name for the German invasion of the Soviet Union in June 1941. Thus, "Operation Barbarossa."

barn yields The actual measure of a crop (for example, grain) harvested and stored, to be contrasted with estimates of the yield made prior to harvest, a procedure followed during Stalin's rule. See **biological yields.**

base See **superstructure and base.**

Battle of Stalingrad The Soviet defeat of the German army at Stalingrad in February 1943 marked a major turning point of World War II in favor of the Allies. Ironically, after 1956 the city was renamed Volgograd.

Berezka Also, *Beriozka.* See **hard currency shops.**

Beriozka Also, **Berezka.** See **hard currency shops.**

Berlin Airlift In response to the Berlin Blockade of April 1948, a massive airlift of food and fuel by the Western Allies kept the city from collapsing, until the blockade was lifted in September 1949.

Berlin Blockade From April 1948 through September 1949, Soviet forces blocked all passage of surface transport into Berlin from the West.

Berlin Treaty (1926) Nonaggression pact between the Soviet Union and Germany. Disturbed by being left out of the Locarno Conference of 1924, Soviet leaders initiated an agreement with Germany. See **"unholy alliance."**

biological yields Reports of yields based upon estimates of potential harvest while the grain is still growing in the fields. In Stalin's day, such reports resulted in greatly inflated, official Soviet crop statistics. See **barn yields.**

black earth (chernozem) The band of rich, black soil stretching across the southwestern region of the USSR.

blat Pull, protection. Illegal string pulling. Deriving favors or goods through bribery, gifts, entertainment, returned favors, under-the-counter exchange, and so forth. The method that enables the tolkachi (expediters) to obtain supplies of raw materials not easily acquired because of bottlenecks in the Soviet planned economy. See **tolkach.**

Bloody Sunday January 22, 1905. St. Petersburg workers, led by Father Gapon, marched peacefully to the Winter Palace to present a petition to the tsar. They were fired upon, and casualties ran to the hundreds or thousands, depending on one's source.

boarding schools (internaty) Schools in which students live full time. They are believed to produce superior Soviet citizens.

Bolsheviki From *bolshinstvo* meaning majority. A radical group within the Social Democratic Labor Party which, under Lenin's leadership, gained supremacy in 1903 and called themselves the Communist Party. They staged the November 1917 Revolution and formed the Soviet Union.

bonuses Salary premia paid to workers for overfulfilling plan.

bourgeois falsifiers A soviet term applied to non-Soviet specialists on the USSR who, assertedly, lie about the nature of the Soviet system, Marxism-Leninism, Soviet foreign relations, and so forth.

bourgeois objectivism An accusation leveled at intellectuals, in all branches of learning, who do not follow the party line in the "ideological rearmament" of the Soviet peoples. Such intellectuals are accused of being apolitical or harmfully objective in their viewpoint and analysis.

bourgeoisie In Soviet terms, the relatively wealthy segment of a capitalist society that lives by exploiting the proletariat and profits from the surplus value of its labor. This class not only controls but also maintains ownership of the means of production and is the source of the exploitation of the workers.

Brest-Litovsk, Treaty of An unequal treaty signed by the Soviet government in March 1918 giving Imperial Germany substantial territorial concessions in the West, including the Ukraine. For Lenin it was an unjust peace imposed upon a weak Soviet state; the treaty would be set aside when the "correlation of forces" created the first opportunity.

Brezhnev Doctrine In justification of the Soviet military action that halted the Czechoslovakian uprising in 1968, Brezhnev declared that once a state had achieved the state of "socialism," it could not be allowed to retrogress to a lower sociopolitical form. Thus, the Soviet Union had the right, indeed a "sacred duty" to prevent other states from retrogressing from socialism, once they had achieved that advanced stage of development. See **Czech Spring.**

brigade A work unit in either industry or agriculture, often constituting a hundred or more workers.

bureau A party organization's steering committee.

bureaucracy A system in which the government machinery is implemented by a professional group of officials who sometimes impede performance through infighting and indolence. In *State and Revolution,* Lenin proposed that under socialism and the withering away of the state, such professionals would be replaced by citizen-volunteers. As in many other countries, "bureaucracy" is used as a derogatory term for an unresponsive state apparatus. Soviet officials, performing their duties under the party's direction are, by definition, not bureaucrats.

Cadet (Kadet) Nickname given to a member of the Constitutional Democratic Party; taken from the party's initials K. D.

Cadet Party; *Kadet Party* Constitutional Democratic Party. Formed in 1905, this moderately left-wing group gained peasant support for its desire to establish a constitutional monarchy. They played an important role in the Provisional Government but were outlawed after the Bolsheviks gained power.

cadre (kadre) The key line personnel of an organization. Stalin said, "Cadres decide everything."

candidate (kandidat) An individual who has completed a university degree and three additional years of study as well as a thesis. Kandidat status is very prestigious in the Soviet Union. Also, most new party members and many new appointees to higher posts (for example, the Central Committee or the Politburo) first enter such bodies as apprentice, nonvoting candidate members.

candidate of science (kandidat nauk) The lowest Soviet graduate degree.

capital accumulation A Marxist doctrine holding that capitalist owners inevitably strive to acquire as much capital as possible.

capitalism According to Marxism, a sociopolitical system determined by private property ownership, and characterized by the exploitation of the working class. All human behavioral ills arise from the exploitation of man by man; exploitation, in turn, is rooted in private ownership of the means of production. Thus, private property is the source of all human evil.

capitalist encirclement A term coined by Stalin to indicate that the USSR was surrounded by unfriendly powers.

card exchanges See **party card.**

CCTU See **Central Council of Trade Unions.**

cell See **primary party organization.**

CEMA Also *CMEA* or *COMECON* See **Council for Mutual Economic Assistance.**

censorship Although all media outlets have attached one or more individuals responsible for censoring material if deemed necessary, self-censorship seems to be the primary means of control over the written and spoken word. See **index; Union of Soviet Writers.**

centner A metric unit of weight (100 kilograms or 220.46 pounds) used in measuring farm yields. A *quintal.*

central apparatus The Moscow-based major organs of the party.

Central Auditing Commission A Moscow-based organ of the party primarily responsible for supervising finances and the efficiency of the party apparatus.

Central Committee of the CPSU Theoretically, the highest organ of the party when a congress is not meeting. The Politburo is the executive committee of the Central Committee.

Central Council of Trade Unions CCTU. The Moscow-based directorate for all trade unions.

central planning The substitution of national economic plans for the marketplace as the guide for all economic activity. See five-year plan; Gosplan.

Central Statistical Administration An arm of the Council of Ministers primarily responsible for collecting and providing economic and social statistical data.

chairman of the Council of Ministers The rough Soviet equivalent of a Western prime minister. See **Council of Ministers.**

chairman of the Presidium of the Supreme Soviet The rough equivalent of a Western president. See **Presidium of the Supreme Soviet.**

Cheka (Chrezvychainaia komissiia po borbe c kontrrevoliutsiei i sabotazhem) The Extraordinary Commission for Combatting Counterrevolution and Sabotage. Created by Lenin in December 1917, this was the first name of the Soviet secret police.

Chekist A member of the Cheka and generally any member of the Soviet security organs (secret police) who works in the manner of "Iron Felix Dzerzhinsky," the first head of the Cheka who was famous for his ruthlessness and cruelty.

Chernobyl A town near Kiev where in late April 1986 a nuclear reactor went out of control and burned, resulting in the death of some thirty people and widespread radioactive contamination.

chernozem See **black earth.**

chief administration The major departmental division of a ministry.

chistka Cleansing or purge. Used by the communists to refer to periodic cleaning out of party ranks of those who do not deserve membership. Under Stalin, it came to mean the removal and elimination of all hostile or potentially hostile elements in the party and society, taking on the form of mass terror.

Chronicle of Current Events An underground journal devoted to alleged Soviet violations of human rights. See **samizdat.**

circle of misery The Marxist doctrine that under capitalism the lot of the workers is destined inevitably to become increasingly miserable.

Civil War, the The 1918–21 Russian Civil War between the Bolsheviks and the White forces. Also see **War Communism.**

class consciousness The Marxist belief that the workers under capitalism, caught in the common trap of increasing misery, evolve a shared sense of their exploitation that eventually will drive them to revolutionary action.

class warfare The most fundamental of all Marxist-Leninist doctrines is that all evil in the world emanates from the exploitation of the proletariat by the bourgeoisie. This phenomenon is said to produce a struggle by the workers for their freedom, the destruction of the bourgeoisie and capitalist exploitation, and the onset of the dictatorship of the proletariat, socialism, and, eventually communism.

classes Assertedly, within the USSR there are only two friendly classes: workers and peasants. Outside of the "socialist" nations there are, assertedly, three major classes: the peasants, the proletariat (workers), and the bourgeoisie, with the latter two in fundamental conflict.

client state A Western term designating a state that is closely allied politically and economically with the USSR. The term was originally applied to East European states, but now includes Cuba, Nicaragua, North Korea, and Vietnam.

CMEA Also *CEMA* or *COMECON*. See **Council for Mutual Economic Assistance.**

coexistence See **peaceful coexistence.**

cold war The state of strained relations that developed between the USSR and its former allies, especially the United States, after World War II.

collective (kollektiv) Every individual in the Soviet Union is regarded as an integral part of his or her local work or living group as well as a member of the larger collective that comprises the whole of Soviet society.

collective competition See **socialist competition.**

collective contract (kollektivnyi podriad) Pushed by Gorbachev and endorsed by the politburo in 1983, this is a scheme designed to increase worker output, especially on the farms. Essentially, groups of workers sign a contract with the parent enterprise to manage and perform a specified portion of the enterprise's work for agreed-upon costs and remuneration. Thus, profits realized from savings on costs or increased production accrue to the workers' benefit.

collective farm (kolkhoz) Agricultural artel. One of the huge "cooperative" farms that account for about half of Soviet farms. Although theoretically they are managed internally, in practice they are closely dominated by outside party directives. Today, the major practical difference between the kolkhozy and the sovkhozy (state farms) is that the workers on the latter are salaried state employees, which the kolkhoz workers are not.

collective leadership Theoretically, this embodies the supreme decision-making authority of the Politburo, which is shared among its members rather than being commandeered by any one individual, as was the case during Stalin's leadership.

collective power of the masses A Marxist doctrine asserting that the power of an entire group is greater than the sum of the power of that group's individual members.

collectivization of agriculture A process, initiated by Stalin in 1929, of consolidating small peasant holdings into state and collective farms, thereby bringing the means of agricultural production under state ownership and control. It may be further interpreted as a method of grain collection. See **collective farm; forced collectivization.**

collegium An advisory body of experts, usually drawn from outside the ministry they serve.

combine See **kombinat.**

COMECON Also *CEMA* or *CEMEA*. See **Council for Mutual Economic Assistance.**

Cominform The Communist Information Bureau. A successor to the Comintern, this Moscow-dominated organization of communist parties existed from 1947 until its demise in 1956. One of its major goals was that of fighting "deviationism," especially "Titoism."

Comintern The Third Communist International, a Moscow-dominated international organization of communists founded by Lenin in 1917 when he became disenchanted with the Second Socialist International. Its purpose was to control the international working class movement and further the world revolution. Parties were admitted to membership only if they accepted the twenty-one conditions laid down by its Second Congress in 1920. Under Stalin it became an adjunct of Soviet foreign policy, and its members were expected to practice "Soviet patriotism." It was dissolved in 1943 as a gesture to the Western Allies.

command economy A Western term used to describe centrally planned economies, which lack such features as free markets and market-determined prices.

commanding heights That 20 percent of Soviet industrial enterprises (employing some 80 percent of the industrial workers) that was not denationalized during the NEP period.

commissar The title (now outmoded) formerly given to heads of Soviet government organs, including posts now held by ministers.

commissariat Central government agencies in the early years. In 1946 the name "ministry" was introduced.

committees of the poor Groups of poor peasants (some of questionable character) organized by party zealots to requisition grain from the kulaks by any means necessary and to stir up resentment toward these relatively well-to-do peasants. The committees were first used by Lenin during the period of War Communism and again by Stalin to achieve forced collectivization in the late 1920s and early 1930s. See **kulak.**

commodities Goods, merchandise. Marx argued that workers' labor, like all other goods, was bought for the lowest possible price in the capitalist markets. Therefore, the Marxists believe that, under capitalism, laborers are commodities.

communal man The Marxian belief that, basically, human beings want to share all material goods with their fellows. This, supposedly, was the original state of humanity in nature until societies were perverted by the corrupting influence of the ownership of means of production.

commune A group of people living and working together, holding all goods in common and owning no private property. Theoretically, to the communist, this is the most perfect human relationship, although in recent times the Soviets rejected as reactionary its use in China under Mao. Also, the village organization under the tsars. See **mir.**

communism Marxism or Marxism-Leninism. The asserted, inevitable, scientific outgrowth of dialectical materialism. It is a level of social development in which private property will no longer exist; all of humanity will share equally in the ownership of the means of production, and thus selfishness, rancor, and human conflict will disappear in the new classless, stateless society.

communism with a human face This term refers to the reform movement within the Czechoslovak Communist Party in 1968, which was ended by the Soviet–Warsaw Pact military intervention in August 1968.

Communist International See **Comintern.**

Communist Manifesto Marx and Engels's 1848 call to revolution. It summarized their theory of dialectical materialism and proclaimed the ultimate overthrow of capitalist society by a worldwide, working-class revolution.

Communist Party of the Soviet Union CPSU. The only legal political party in the Soviet Union. Its members dominate all spheres of human activity in the USSR.

Communist Youth League See **Young Communist League.**

Composers' Union See **creative unions; Union of Soviet Composers.**

comrades' courts Below and outside the state court system, these quasi-legal institutions, composed of workers and peasants, employ criticism and self-criticism along with small fines or penalties in an effort to shape attitudes and behavior along desirable "socialist" lines.

Congress of the CPSU Theoretically, the ruling body of the Communist Party of the Soviet Union. Periodically (usually every five years) several thousand "elected" delegates convene for a few days in Moscow to approve new party programs and rules. Dominated by the Politburo, the Central Committee provides leadership between the congresses. In practice, the congresses are largely ceremonial and legitimizing events.

Constituent Assembly A body elected in November 1917 and charged primarily with creating a new constitutional system of government. The Bolsheviks forcefully dissolved it after only one session, in January 1918.

Constitution Assertedly the "fundamental law" of the Soviet Union. The first RSFSR Constitution was promulgated in 1918. The second, the Stalin Constitution, was adopted in 1936, and the current Constitution came into force in 1977. Most Westerners regard it as primarily a programatic document, but not one that restricts the powers of the government or the party.

Constitutional Democratic Party See **Cadet Party.**

containment policy A U.S. policy initiated under Truman to resist Soviet expansion.

convergence theory A view shared by both Soviet and some Western analysts that the forces of modern society are destined to bring communist and noncommunist systems together. However, whereas the Soviet analysts believe that the communist model will triumph essentially, many Western convergence theorists believe that the forces of change will diminish the rigidities and controls existing in the USSR.

corrective labor camps Concentration camps that utilized forced labor on various projects. At the peak of their use, under Stalin, they are estimated to have contained at least several million inmates. Apparently they were largely phased out in 1956 and replaced by corrective labor colonies. Solzhenitsyn's *Gulag Archipelago* describes these camps.

corrective labor colonies Assertedly more benign than the corrective labor camps, this institution also uses inmate labor on various projects.

correlation of forces The Soviet concept of the dynamic relationship affecting the struggle between opposing social forces. In the international realm, the concept embraces all sources of power (political, economic, social, ideological, and military) that comprise a moving balance of power between capitalism and communism, one that is ultimately tilted towards the inevitable world revolution. Therefore, although the Soviets will agree that at any moment in time the correlation may not be favorable to the advancement of world communism, in the long run, the general trend is in that direction.

cossacks An ethnic group of freemen, famous for their horsemanship, who lived on the southern and eastern frontiers of the empire during tsarist times. Through a process of "regularization" in the late eighteenth and early nineteenth centuries, this group was transformed into a loyal military caste that served the tsars as light cavalry and an internal police force for dealing with unrest.

Council for Mutual Economic Assistance Also *CEMA, CMEA,* or *COMECON*; CMEA is the official abbreviation. The council was formed in 1949 to enhance socialist international cooperation. Its members are Bulgaria, Cuba, Czechoslovakia, the German Democratic Republic, Hungary, Mongolia, Poland, Romania, the USSR, and Vietnam. Observers are Afghanistan, Angola, Ethiopia, Laos, Mexico, Mozambique, Nicaragua, and the People's Democratic Republic of Yemen.

Council of Ministers According to the Soviet Constitution, the "highest executive and administration body" of the USSR. In practice, its members direct most day-to-day state activities. It is divided into two bodies: The Council of the Republics and The Council of the Union. The chairman of the Council of Ministers is a rough equivalent of a Western prime minister.

Council of People's Commissars In the early years, the name of the leading group of government administrators, later changed to Council of Ministers.

Council of Nationalities See **Soviet of Nationalities.**

Council of the Union See **Soviet of the Union.**

counterrevolutionary Also *KRs.* A term directed against anyone within the communist system who is suspected of wishing to change it. Used especially during the NEP period, it has been variously applied to the one-time Cadets who supported rightist parties in the revolutionary period, and to tsarist bureaucrats, White Guards, priests, landowners, nobility, and industrialists.

CPSU See **Communist Party of the Soviet Union.**

CPSU(b) Communist Party of the Soviet Union (Bolshevik). In the early years of Soviet rule the (b) was added to

CPSU to distinguish the Bolshevik Party from other groups, especially the Mensheviks. In 1952 the "Bolshevik" was dropped.

creative unions Organizations of creative artists. See **Union of Soviet Composers; Union of Soviet Writers.**

criticism and self-criticism (kritika i samokritika) The widespread practice of publicly admitting (for example, at a union meeting) one's own faults and shortcomings and/or accusing one's colleagues of failures.

Cuban missile crisis The serious standoff between Khrushchev and Kennedy during October 1962 when U.S. U-2 planes discovered that the USSR was installing intermediate-range ballistic missiles in Cuba.

cult of personality (kult lichnosti) The attribution of superhuman powers and wisdom to an individual. Stalin, and later Khrushchev, were accused of encouraging such attitudes, abusing the office of general secretary, acting too arbitrarily, and violating the principle of collective leadership by making themselves supreme in every sphere.

cultural revolution An effort in the late 1920s and early 1930s to raise the educational level and the cultural interests of the workers and peasants.

Czech Spring A Western description for the ill-fated period of Czechoslovakian reform and revitalization in 1968 that was ended by Soviet and Warsaw Pact military intervention. That intervention heralded the establishment of the **Brezhnev Doctrine,** which see.

dacha A summer cottage in the country. A major perquisite available to important Soviet officials.

Decembrists (dekabristy) Officers and noblemen who took part in an uprising against tsarism and for a constitution in December 1825. Upon their return from Western Europe after the Napoleonic Wars, these men formed secret societies, and worked for enlightenment and reform.

But they despaired of any hope in their government, and they rose in 1825. Many historians see the uprising as but the first of many such events that eventually culminated in the downfall of tsardom.

Defense Council (Soviet oborony) The chief decision-making organ of the Soviet national security apparatus, composed of selected members of the Politburo and headed by the general secretary of the party and the president of the Presidium. The chief of the general staff is believed to serve as rapporteur for this body.

dekulakization (raskulachivanie) Stalin's decreed destruction of the well-to-do peasants. The Russian word means to tear the kulaks out by the roots. See **kulak.**

democracy According to the Soviets, socialist democracy is the only genuine democracy. In Marxist-Leninist theory, there is no democracy except under communism. The emphasis is on equality—especially economic equality, which is defined as all having the same relationship to the means of production. See **freedom.**

democratic centralism A Leninist doctrine. Free discussion and deliberation of all issues by the party or involved public until a decision is made. Once the decision is made, it becomes law and every member follows it. No further discussion is tolerated except on the means of carrying out the plan. Lenin called it "freedom to criticize and unity in action."

democratic centralists A group of high-ranking party members who, in the 1919–22 period, unsuccessfully opposed Lenin's interpretation of democratic centralism, favoring instead a more democratic approach.

deputies Representatives to the various soviets.

de-Stalinization The criticism of some of Stalin's actions and the rejection of some of his practices, especially the use of mass terror as a key element of rule. De-Stalinization was initiated largely by Khrushchev's so-called secret speech in 1956.

détente (razriadka) During the 1970s, both Soviet and U.S. diplomats agreed that a new level of discussion and exchanges had been reached, a level higher than "peaceful coexistence"—thus "détente."

detskii sad Kindergartens or day child-care centers for the very young.

developed socialism See **advanced socialism.**

deviation Aberration from prescribed attitudes or behavior, including both revision and dogmatism as deviations of the left and right. This is a major sin in the USSR, where under democratic centralism, all are required to adhere rigidly to any policy once it has been decided upon.

dialectical materialism The wedding by Marx and Engels of key aspects of historical materialism to principles of Hegel's dialectic. So constituted, for them the human equation became a class struggle between the thesis (bourgeois capitalist society) and the antithesis (the exploited proletarian workers), that would produce a new synthesis, that is, a dictatorship of the proletariat that would evolve into socialism and, ultimately, communism.

dialectics A method of logic used by Hegel and based on contradiction of opposites (thesis and antithesis) and their continual resolution (synthesis). Marx adapted this to historical materialism.

dictatorship of the bourgeoisie The asserted dominance of the capitalist class through a system of repression of the workers. See **bourgeoisie.**

dictatorship of the proletariat The early stage of societal organization after the overthrow of capitalism involving the dominance of the workers to suppress counterrevolutionary resistance of the exploiting class. Thus, the early stage of Soviet rule, when the party staked out its claim to embody the will of the workers. See **counterrevolutionary.**

director's fund A small amount of the profits of an enterprise that the director is allowed to spend at his or her discretion for the improvement of that enterprise.

discipline See **party discipline; socialist discipline.**

dissident (inakomysliashchii) Different minded. An individual who thinks differently, who holds and expresses important beliefs that run counter to official doctrine or policy.

"dizzy with success" Also *"dizziness with success."* Fearing that the excesses of some party zealots during the early months of the "forced collectivization" drive were damaging the cause, Stalin gave a speech in 1930 warning that some of the colleagues were going too fast and too far and were becoming "dizzy" with apparent successes. This was a tactical retreat and not a rejection from the general line of forced collectivization.

doctor of sciences (doktor nauk) The highest Soviet graduate degree.

Doctors' Plot An alleged plot among the Kremlin doctors (mostly Jewish) to cut short the lives of Zhdanov and Shcherbakov and to undermine the health of the military. Construed as a threat on Stalin's life, it set the stage for another bloody, mass purge with anti-Semitic overtones. The "plot" was exposed by Stalin in 1952 and rejected as untrue after his death.

dogmatism A cardinal communist sin is to resist doctrinal changes made necessary by shifts in the objective conditions and the correlation of forces. The "science of Marxism-Leninism" demands a unity of theory and practice in flexible, not ossified, doctrine.

DOSAAF (Dobrovolnoe obshchestvo sodeistviia armii, aviatsii i flotu) The civilian Voluntary Society for Assistance to the Army, Air Force, and Navy. It also engages in civil defense and paramilitary activities.

druzhini See **voluntary militia.**

dual power (dvoevlastie) Lenin's description of the political situation in Russia following the February revolution, in which two centers of power existed, the Provisional Government and the soviets. In the April Theses Lenin called for the ending of dual power through the overthrow of the Provisional Government.

Duma The lower house of the tsarist legislature, created in October 1905. The upper house consisted of the reorganized State Council.

dvor A household in tsarist Russia.

Eastern Locarnos Stimulated by the Locarno Treaty of 1924 and patterned after the Berlin Treaty of 1926, a series of mutual understanding, nonagression pacts were initiated in the late 1920s by Soviet leaders with their neighbors.

economism The view held by an influential group of social democrats in the late 1800s that the proletariat should stay out of political affairs, which tended to divide them, and concentrate all efforts on trade union activities. Lenin strongly opposed this attitude.

edinonachalie See **one-man management.**

elections Although the USSR has local and national balloting for state offices, before Gorbachev's rise to power, only one candidate ever appeared on the ballot for each office, and that individual had to be approved by the party. Beginning in 1987 there have been some instances of multiple candidates at the local level. Election day is a national holiday. Voter turnout is very high because elections are a form of political participation and a legitimizing device; thus, going to the polls is the proper thing to do.

elitism Western analysts assert that Soviet party members constitute a political elite and that elitism is a key aspect of the Soviet system of rule.

emancipation See **peasant emancipation.**

ethnic minorities The minority nationality groups in the USSR. The Soviet Union is populated by Russians (approximately half of the population) plus several score of other nationality groups, most of which are non-Slavic people.

Eurocommunism This is a Western term applied to European-style communism that arose in the 1970s. Its adherents claim to believe in communism, but to one degree or another express disagreement with the Soviet line. See **polycentrism,** which was a root of Eurocommunism.

expatriate One who has left his or her native country and resides in another.

factionalism The illegal formation of dissenting groups within any official government or party group. Factionalism was outlawed by the Tenth Party Congress in 1921 as a breach of party discipline.

faculty (fakultet) A school or division of a university.

fascism The form of rigid, one-party dictatorship that originated in Italy in 1922. Applied especially to Franco's Spain, Mussolini's Italy, and Hitler's Germany. Used by Marxist-Leninists as the ultimate epithet for the bourgeoisie. They believe that all capitalist systems are destined to evolve into extreme, exploitative, dictatorial systems.

February Revolution In February 1917 Tsar Nicholas II abdicated, the old system collapsed, and the Provisional Government assumed control.

federal system Theoretically, the Soviet system of government follows the U.S. model, with important governmental powers reserved for geographically defined political subdivisions—that is, the republics. In practice, the republics have few residual powers.

fellow traveler A term first used in the 1920s by Russian party members to designate individuals, especially intellectuals, who were positive toward the Soviet system although they were not members of a communist party. Later used in the West to designate communist sympathizers.

ferma The livestock section of a collective farm.

feuilleton A brief commentary on, or criticism of, some aspect of Soviet life, carried in the central newspapers.

Finlandization A Western term applied to the political neutralization of Finland. The term describes any country that accedes, especially in the foreign policy realm, to Soviet desires.

"first commandment" That which has the highest policy priority. During most of Stalin's rule the "first commandment" was "highest priority to industrial construction."

First Great Imperialist War, the According to Marxist-Leninist theory all modern wars stem from the inevitability of capitalist imperialism. Thus this title for World War I.

First International The International Working Men's Association founded by Marx in London in 1864. It collapsed in 1873 after the fall of the Paris Commune of 1870–71.

first secretaries Each party unit at every level (for example, republic, oblast, and raion) is led by a first secretary. At the national level, before 1953 and after 1966, the leading secretary has also had the title general secretary.

five-year plan Every five years a comprehensive plan is created that establishes the nation's economic goals for the subsequent five-year period. In the USSR, once plans are outlined they are regarded as law, and there is a tendency to assume that they will be achieved automatically. The Twelfth Five-Year Plan is for the 1986–90 period. See **Gosplan; planned economy; planning.**

food program, the This is a set of policies and guidelines (introduced in 1980) designed to improve the quantity and quality of food in the USSR. It includes administrative reorganization and increased support to the agro-industrial complex.

forced collectivization Although Soviet authorities never admit that force was used in the collectivization of agriculture initiated at the end of the 1920s, Stalin did refer to the collectivization drive as a "revolution from above." See **collectivization of agriculture; dekulakization.**

forced industrialization Under Stalin all priority was given to the most rapid construction possible of industry, especially heavy industry. See **"first commandment."**

formalism Originally, a school of literary theory beginning in the early 1900s that focused on technique and device. The school was politically condemned in 1930, and its followers were persecuted under Stalin. Since that time the word "formalism" has been applied to art forms—esepcially Western trends in music—that do not meet with party-prescribed qualifications. See **socialist realism.**

freedom "The perception of necessity" is a phrase used repeatedly by Soviet political philosophers. According to Soviet doctrine, one can be free only if one behaves according to the dictates of the Marxist-Leninist "science of society." Therefore, freedom consists of acknowledging those dictates and choosing to follow them.

general crisis of capitalism The period beginning with World War I marking the asserted "revolutionary collapse of capitalism."

general meeting The central concept of "kolkhoz democracy." Theoretically, all key decisions made on the collective farms are made by the members in periodic general meetings. In practice, the members rubber-stamp whatever the farm leadership puts before them.

general secretary The first secretary of the Central Committee of the Communist Party of the Soviet Union and the chairman of the Politburo. The top-ranking official in the CPSU and, hence, the leader of the country. From 1953 to 1966 called "first secretary."

generalnyi prokuror SSR See **procurator general.**

gigantomania A Russian term, used mostly by Westerners, that describes the Russian feeling of expansiveness that seems to arise out of an awe for the vast reaches of Russian land. The term now probably incorporates the communist tendency to regard large industrial and agricultural enterprises as inherently superior to smaller enterprises.

glasnost See **openness.**

glav Chief or main.

glavk (glavnyi komitet) Central directorate. The department of a ministry controlling either a branch of industry falling within the competence of the ministry or establishments in a particular area.

Glavlit Chief Administration of Literary and Publishing Affairs. It plays a key role in the system of press control by working to guarantee that all literature remains true to "party mindedness." See **socialist realism.**

glavnoe upravlenie Chief administration.

globalistika Globalistics, the systematic study of worldwide trends in order to make forecasts of future developments. It is an expanded field of study in the USSR and is part of the ideological struggle against bourgeois futurism.

Goelro (Gosudarstvennaia komissiia po elektrifikatsii Rossii) The State Commission for the Electrification of Russia (a plan formulated in 1920), out of which grew Gosplan.

gor (from gorodskoi) The Russian prefix for city.

gorispolkom (gorodskoi ispolnitelnyi komitet) The executive committee of a city soviet.

gorkom (gorodskoi komitet) The city party committee.

gorod City.

gorraikom (gorodskoi-raionnyi komitet) An urban district (raion) party committee.

gos (from gosudarstvennyi) The Russian prefix for state.

Gosagroprom (Gosudarstvennyi agro-promyshlennyi kompleks) The central organ of the agro-industrial complex.

Gosarbitrazh (Gosudarstvennyi arbitrazh) The state arbitration court that encompasses all government enterprises and institutions and resolves disputes between such organizations.

Gosbank The state bank.

Gosplan The Soviet State Planning Commission that under party guidance is primarily responsible for creating the five-year plans. See **five-year plan; planned economy; planning.**

Gosstroi (Gosudarstvennyi komitet po delam stroitelstva) The USSR State Committee for Construction.

Gosteleradio (Gosudarstvennyi komitet Soveta ministrov SSSR po televideniiu i radioveshchaniiu) The State Committee of the USSR Council of Ministers for Television and Radiobroadcasting.

GPU (Gosudarstvennoe politicheskoe upravlenie) See **state political administration.**

great october A Soviet reference to the 1917 beginning of the Bolshevik Revolution.

Great Patriotic War The Soviet name for World War II, also known as the "Second Great Imperialist War."

Great Purge, the See **purge.**

Gregorian calendar See **Julian calendar.**

GTO (Gotov k trudu i oborone) "Ready for labor and defense." Program of mass mobilization of Soviet youth for labor and military service.

Gulag (Glavnoe upravlenie ispravitelno-trudovykh lagerei) The main administration of the corrective labor camps.

Gulag archipelago Title of Solzhenitsyn's book describing the penal camps. See **corrective labor camps; Gulag.**

hammer and sickle The official Soviet symbol of a crossed hammer and sickle as emblazoned on the Soviet flag. The hammer symbolizes the workers; the sickle, the peasants; and the fact that they are crossed symbolizes worker–peasant unity.

hard currency Any international currency that is freely exchangeable across national boundaries. The Soviet authorities prohibit the exchange of the ruble and forbid its export.

hard currency shops The *Berezka* or *Beriozka.* Always short of hard currency for foreign purchases, Soviet authorities have located stores, filled largely with souvenir goods, in or near Intourist hotels, where purchases can be made only with convertible currencies, for example, dollars, pounds, marks, and other Western currencies.

hectare A unit of land measure. One hectare equals 2.471 acres.

Helsinki Accords Agreements concluded by NATO, the Warsaw Pact, and neutral and nonaligned nations at the Helsinki Conference on Security and Cooperation in Europe. The Helsinki Final Act was signed in 1975. Within the three so-called "baskets" of agreements was a recognition by the West of the post–World War II Eastern European boundaries and the Soviet agreement to promote human rights, among them the free flow of people and ideas.

Helsinki watch groups Groups originally formed in Lithuania to report on the violations of the human-rights provisions of the Helsinki Accords.

Heroine Mother An award given to women who have given birth to at least ten children.

higher party schools See **party schools.**

historical materialism A Marxian doctrine holding that all human activity and behavior is rooted in the physical, three-dimensional realm.

honeymoon of the Revolution The few weeks of relative calm between the 1917 Bolshevik takeover and the outbreak of the Civil War. It was a period of much euphoria when many believed that the blessings of communism were just around the corner.

hooliganism (khuliganstvo) As defined in the criminal codes, "intentional actions violating public order in a coarse manner and expressing a clear disrespect for society." Thus, hooliganism is unacceptable, deviant public behavior, especially on the part of youth.

Hungarian uprising In October 1956, following on the heels of Khrushchev's de-Stalinization speech, large numbers of Hungarian citizens revolted. The nationalist Premier Imre Nagy declared the abandonment of a one-party state and that Hungary would leave the Warsaw Pact. However, Soviet tanks squelched the revolt; Nagy was executed in 1958.

icon A painting, usually on wood, of holy figures, used for worship in the Russian Orthodox church and in homes of believers.

icon corner (krasnyi kut or krasnyi ugol) Literally, beautiful corner. A corner in a Russian Orthodox believer's home containing an icon and candles on a small table. This corner, like an altar, is reserved for prayer and worship. Kut is an archaic church term, but still in use.

ideological struggle A Soviet notion that in the world of ideas there is a battle being waged between capitalism and socialism. Therefore, no ideas are value-neutral or objective in and of themselves.

ideology, Marxist The total body of the asserted "laws of society" ascribed to Marx, Engels, and Lenin. Thus, Marxism-Leninism.

imperialism According to Lenin, "the highest stage of capitalism, . . . the last, all-encompassing stage of capitalism just before its collapse."

income tax See **taxes.**

increasing circle of misery See **circle of misery.**

index A directory of subjects that are not to be published without approval by higher authority (for example, reports on natural disasters, strikes, comparisons of Soviet and Western standards). The index is supplied to every journal editor, radio, or TV director. See **talmud.**

inevitability of war doctrine Although rejected in recent years by Soviet theorists, most Western analysts agree that a major thrust of Lenin's writing was the inevitability of war between communist and capitalist states.

initsiativniki An illegal splinter group of Soviet Baptists.

inspector organizers Local party officials originally attached to the MTS (machine tractor stations) and responsible for monitoring the work of several farms in the district. Now they are attached to the raion office.

institute An advanced professional school or research facility.

intelligentsiia White-collar workers above the clerical level, independent professional people, and intellectuals.

internal passport All adult Soviet citizens are required to carry official identification papers, and to present them to officials upon request. Thus, the passport is essential for travel within the USSR.

international brigades Units made up largely of people with socialist or communist convictions who volunteered to fight in the 1936–39 Spanish Civil War on the Soviet-backed Republican side against Franco's forces.

international communist movement See **internationalism; world revolutionary forces.**

International Department An organ of the Central Committee believed to be important in foreign policy matters.

international workers' movement The Marxist-Leninist belief that there is a strong bond among the world's workers that creates an international class consciousness that will lead to the eventual world communist revolution. See **internationalism; world revolutionary forces.**

internationalism A Marxist-Leninist belief that the workers of the world are bound together by a common bond that supplants nationalism. Also, the commitment of communists to eventual world communism, including the obligation to do everything to facilitate its genesis.

internationals See **Comintern; First International; Second International.**

internaty See **boarding schools.**

intervention See **allied intervention.**

Intourist (Intourist) The Soviet state tourist agency that manages the travel of foreigners inside the USSR.

iron curtain Churchill's description of the informational and physical barriers erected by the USSR to block the flow of human beings and ideas between the Soviet Union and the outside world. Thus, from the Baltic to the Adriatic, "an iron curtain has descended across the Continent" (Winston Churchill, Fulton, Missouri, 5 March 1946).

Iskra *The Spark.* The name of the first illegal Marxist newspaper published in the Russian language, based on Leninist thought. Lenin supervised the publication of the first issue at the end of 1900 in Munich. During its first years the journal was a major sounding board for Lenin's ideas.

iskra theory A Bolshevik idea that staging a communist takeover in Russia would spark an immediate communist revolution among the exploited war-weary masses of Europe.

ispolkom (ispolnitelnyi komitet) An executive committee.

Izvestiia *News.* The name of the leading Soviet state newspaper. The organ of the USSR Council of Ministers.

Jackson–Vanik amendment Legislation in the U.S. Senate in the mid-1970s that tied cooperation with the USSR to Soviet compliance with the human-rights provisions of the Helsinki agreements. As a result many Soviet Jews were allowed to leave the USSR. See **Helsinki Accords; Stevenson amendment.**

Jewish railroad A Western term used to describe a method of emigration from the USSR in the 1970s and 1980s. With the relaxation of restrictions on the emigration of Jews, many Soviet citizens used their claim of being Jewish (whether they actually were or not) to obtain exit visas to Israel, although that state often was not their intended ultimate destination.

Julian calendar The Julian calendar (or Old Style) was used in Russia until 1 February 1918 (OS). The calendar was introduced by Julius Caesar in 46 B.C. However, the

Julian year was slightly more than eleven minutes too long. In 1582, Pope Gregory XIII introduced a new calendar that suppressed the ten days that had accrued because of this error, and brought the calendar into closer conformity with astronomical data. Most of the Western world adhered to the Gregorian calendar (or New Style) by the time the Bolsheviks staged their Revolution on 25 October 1917 (OS), or 7 November (NS). On 1 February 1918 (OS), the Bolsheviks introduced the Gregorian calendar (suppressing thirteen days), and that date became 14 February 1918 (NS). The Russian Orthodox church still adheres to the Julian calendar.

July Days, the During a cabinet crisis in the Provisional Government of 1917 (Alexander Kerensky was to replace Prince Georgii Lvov as the head), leftist riots broke out in Petrograd, followed by repressive measures that helped convince Lenin that the only salvation was the creation of a "dictatorship of the proletariat."

Kadet See **Cadet.**

Kadet Party See **Cadet Party.**

kandidat See **candidate.**

Kadre See **Cadre.**

Katyn Forest A forest near Smolensk where the corpses of thousands of missing Polish officers were found in the early 1940s. Most Western analysts believe that the officers were executed by Soviet security forces.

Kellogg–Briand Pact In the effort to avoid war, twenty-three nations signed a 1928 agreement providing for conciliation and arbitration of disputes. The Soviet Union was a signatory, although it felt that provision for disarmament should have been included.

Kerensky, Alexander A right Socialist Revolutionary who served as prime minister under the Provisional Government from July until October 1917. Also spelled Aleksandr Kerenskii.

KGB (Komitet gosudarstvennoi bezopasnosti) The Committee for State Security. The Soviet secret police that was separated from the MVD (internal police) in 1954.

khozraschet Economic or cost accounting. The attempt to put Soviet enterprises on a pay-as-you-go basis.

klassovost Class character or mindedness, arising out of heightened class consciousness. See **socialist realism.**

kolkhoz See **collective farm.**

kolkhoz market (kolkhoznyi rynok) Stalls located in cities and towns where individual peasants sell produce originating chiefly from their private plots, or livestock products derived from peasant private enterprise.

kolkhoznik A member of a collective farm.

kollegiia A board or group of officials who serve as consultants. Also, a group of lawyers.

kombinat An economic enterprise that combines several related enterprises.

Komitetchiki The committee members of the communist underground (Stalin was one) who were the first prototypes of the apparatchiki with whom Stalin was to forge his party machine.

Kommunist The main theoretical journal of the CPSU, named *Bolshevik* prior to 1952.

Komsomol See **Young Communist League.**

Komsomolskaia Pravda The Young Communist League's newspaper.

kopeck (kopeika) The Soviet cent. One one-hundredth of a ruble.

korenizatsiia The policy under Stalin that used people of the "native populations" of the minority nationalities for the area's courts and administrative organs of direct government. Its primary purpose was to facilitate the sovietization of minority peoples through their own native language, culture, and educational systems.

Kornilov affair An aborted attempt in August 1917 led by General Lavr Kornilov to move against the Petrograd Soviet.

KPSS The CPSU. See **Communist Party of the Soviet Union.**

krai A territorial or regional administrative subdivision of a republic. Most often the name applied to such a region is oblast.

kraiispolkom (kraevoi ispolnitelnyi komitet) The executive committee of a krai.

kraikom (kraevoi komitet) The krai party committee.

Krasnaia zvezda *Red Star,* the Soviet military newspaper.

krasnyi kut; krasnyi ugol See **icon corner.**

krasnyi ugolok The Red Corner. A room in factories and offices providing recreational facilities and materials for political propaganda and education.

Kremlin (Kreml) Originally, a fortified complex within a Russian medieval town, containing palaces, churches, and government buildings. The Moscow Kremlin was the seat of power of the centralized Russian state from the fourteenth to the eighteenth centuries. Now the Kremlin is the seat of power of the Soviet Union. Westerners use the term to designate the focus of Soviet political power.

Kremlinology An aspect of Sovietology that attempts to understand the relationships among the top Soviet leaders. This is done through archival research, and by such methods as comparing the content and emphasis of their speeches and by noting who is standing in what place in official pictures taken during major ceremonial occasions—

for example, the line-up on top of Lenin's Tomb when the Politburo reviews the annual May Day parade.

kritika i samokritika See **criticism and self-criticism.**

Krokodil A weekly humor magazine issued by the *Pravda* publishing house. Much of its humor is directed against capitalist societies, but some of its double-entendre jokes and cartoons quite daringly castigate Soviet foibles.

Kronstadt revolt Although sailors at the Kronstadt naval base had been crucial to the success of the Bolshevik coup in Petro-grad against the Provisional Government in October 1917, by 1921 they had become so disillusioned with the new regime that they staged a major, but unsuccessful, revolt under the banner of "Soviets without parties."

KRs See **counter-revolutionary.**

kto kogo A Russian phrase used by Lenin to mean who would do what to whom. The phrase contains no verb but indicates action by the first upon the second. The meaning (whether an indefinite or definite "who does what to whom," or who beats, dominates, or destroys whom) implies struggle for hegemony. Brumberg writes: "The truth of the matter, however, is that this phrase summarized not only the attitude of the Party toward its external enemies, but toward its perennial internal enemies as well" (Abraham Brumberg, ed., *Russia under Khrushchev,* New York: Frederick A. Praeger, 1962, p. 69).

kulak In Russian the word means "tight fist," and in prerevolutionary Russia it was slang for miserly people who enriched themselves through the suffering of others. The Bolsheviks applied it to the peasants who hired labor. But in practice it came to apply to any well-off peasant, and even to some not so well off who were caught in Stalin's drive to destroy the kulaks. Western sources estimate that between five and ten million people died either during the drive or later in the man-made famine that resulted from the disruption of agriculture, especially in the Ukraine. See **dekulization.**

labor book (trudovaia knizhka) Every Soviet worker carries a record of previous employment as provided by management.

labor camps Corrective camps established in 1930 to isolate "socially dangerous" persons and to reform them through labor. Solzhenitsyn's *Gulag Archipelago* describes these camps. The severity of these camps under Stalin has been highly publicized; presumably, they are now less severe and less populated. Much of the USSR was built by such labor.

labor day (trudoden) Work-day units that originally were supposed to be the equivalent of the amount of labor expended in a day by a collective farm worker to complete a specific task. Thus, a piece-work measure. With the post-Stalin adoption of a guaranteed minimum wage for the kolkhozniki, labor-day measurements are no longer used.

labor theory of value An economic doctrine, adopted by Marx, that the value of all commodities and services stems entirely from the amount of labor expended to produce the commodity or to provide the service.

League of Nations Born out of World War I, the league was designed to keep nations from resorting to war to settle their disputes. Although the Soviet Union was not among the original members, it joined in 1934 when, alarmed by the rise of fascism in Germany, the Soviet leaders hoped that the league would provide a shield of collective security. The United States did not join the league.

left communists See **left opposition.**

left opposition The more militant, revolutionary members of the party in the early years. Bukharin was a key leader of the group.

left-wing communism Leninist description of communist romantics who wanted maximum revolutionary changes regardless of the tactical situation.

lend–lease World War II Western aid, especially given by the United States to the USSR.

Lenin Prize The most prestigious award that can be given to Soviet citizens for their achievements in promoting the system and its goals. From 1939 to 1956, the prize was called the *Stalin Prize.*

Leningrad affair Made public by Khrushchev in his 1956 "secret speech," this was a persecution led by Politburo member Malenkov against leading Leningrad officials after the death of Zhdanov in 1948. Zhdanov had been a longtime Leningrad party official, and at one time was thought to be Stalin's closest friend. Apparently, Zhdanov had fallen from Stalin's favor.

Leninism From a Western point of view, the doctrinal additions and changes that Lenin made in Marxism. From the Soviet point of view, Lenin made no fundamental changes in Marxism; he only extended the "science of society," now usually referred to as Marxism-Leninism.

Leninist peaceful coexistence See **peaceful coexistence.**

Lenin's Tomb The mausoleum just outside the Kremlin walls where Lenin's embalmed body is on display. Its roof serves as the reviewing stand for major parades such as the one held each May Day.

Liberman proposals Suggestions first made in 1962 by Evsei Liberman, a prominent Soviet economics professor at the University of Kharkov. He stressed the need to emphasize the profit motive and, by implication, advocated a shift toward a market economy that would reduce the importance of central planning and reduce party control. Very little came of his proposals.

Libermanism See **Liberman proposals.**

link (zveno) A small group, a team. The smallest Soviet collective—for example, a row of students in a classroom or half a dozen or so workers on a farm organized as a working group. The latter would be in contrast with the traditional large-brigade system of organization. See **collective contract.**

linkage A U.S. policy to tie increased trade, cooperation, and the like with the USSR to improved Soviet behavior.

liquidationism A term applied by Lenin to the Menshevik move to abandon the underground party and to concentrate on legal work in the trade unions and the Duma, thereby making the party a broad and open one.

Literaturnaia Gazeta The Union of Soviet Writers' literary magazine.

Little Octobrists A youth organization for children between the ages of seven and ten. The slogan "Only those who love labor can be called Octobrist" (that is, a supporter of the October Revolution), reflects the goal of the party leaders to instill in children a respect for communist tradition and ideology.

localism (mestnye interesy; mestnichestvo) A negative term applied to various activities by local economic or other groups who put their needs above national needs (for example, the encouragement of actions in the economic realm that do not give first priority to meeting the central economic plan).

Locarno Agreement Provisions arising out of the 1924 Locarno Conference designed to secure the Belgian, French, and German borders. The Soviets felt rebuffed by being excluded from the conference. See **Berlin Treaty; Eastern Locarnos.**

London Poles The World War II London-based Polish government-in-exile.

Lvov, Prince Georgii The head of the 1917 Provisional Government until he was succeeded by Kerensky in July.

Lysenkoism The theories of Trofim D. Lysenko, and his reign over Soviet genetics, chiefly in the 1940s and 1950s. This Ukrainian agronomist, now discredited, rejected Mendelian genetics for the Lamarckian view that the environment causes structural changes in plants and animals that are then transmitted to offspring. Reflecting in his theories the wishful thinking of Soviet leaders, Lysenko gained their support. By his long domination of Soviet genetics, he made Soviet biology the laughingstock of scientists the world over.

machine tractor stations (MTS) Until they were abandoned under Khrushchev in 1958, these rural state agencies dominated the Soviet farms. Serving some ten or more farms, they owned all of the major machinery and long served as state agencies for the collection of grain.

Main Political Administration (MPA; Glavnoe politicheskoe upravlenie; GPU) Attached to the Ministry of Defense, this is the party-directed office in charge of education and propaganda as well as the supervision of the Young Communist League and party affairs within the military. The administration directs the political officers, the **zampolity,** which see.

Maoism The teachings and practices of Mao Zedong. Following the Sino-Soviet split, it became a major Soviet epithet signifying serious deviation from "true" Marxism-Leninism.

Marxism The name given to the body of doctrine evolved by Marx and Engels. Although Marx and his followers would argue that they had discovered a "science of society" based upon economic determinism (see **dialectical materialism**), many Western critics assert that this work was primarily sociological, resting on questionable assumptions—for example, that in the state of nature, human relationships are communal.

Marxism-Leninism The body of doctrine that combines Marxist and Leninist thought with emphasis upon the additions made by Lenin. See **communism; Leninism; Marxism.**

mass mobilization The encouragement and propagandizing of the whole society to behave in a desired fashion, for example, to assure plan fulfillment.

mass terror The use of punishment or the threat of punishment to control the population, especially under Stalin. Thus, an essential ingredient of Stalinism. According to Merle Fainsod, mass terror was the "lynchpin" of Soviet rule under Stalin. See **Stalinism.**

masses The working people who, according to Marxism-Leninism, play a decisive role in the development of their society. Therefore, the leaders are merely the people's agents; they can function only with the support of the masses. The masses through their labor power are the key to production.

materialism See **historical materialism.**

May Day May First, the international workers' day. May Day is the major Soviet holiday, complete with a parade in Red Square and the issuance of party and patriotic slogans.

means of production The resources (land, minerals, and so forth) and the tools (factories, machines, and the like) necessary to produce goods. For the Marxist, whoever owns the means of production controls the society.

Menshevik Member of the minority. A political party active from 1903 to 1922. This more liberal group of Social Democrats opted for a large, more democratic party, opposing Lenin and the Bolshevik stand for a tight, disciplined party organization. It was suppressed in the USSR after 1922.

messianism This attitude implies a conviction of superiority along with a commitment to carry a message enthusiastically to the world. Many Western scholars believe that messianism, an ingredient of tsarist Russian thought, has been amalgamated with communist optimism, producing a new Soviet messianism.

mestnichestvo See **localism.**

MGB See **Ministry of State Security.**

militarization of labor An idea propounded by Trotsky that labor should be organized and run like a strict military operation. Labor armies, formerly detachments of the Red Army, were employed in 1920 on heavy work of all kinds.

militarization of society (voenizatsiia obshchestva) Proposals during the 1920s by Red Army commanders, including M. Tukhachevsky, for the militarization of all institutions under party leaders to increase the nation's military preparedness and mobilization capacity.

military commissar See also **politruk.** Refers to party watchdogs appointed to check on military commanders, especially former tsarist officers, during the Civil War. Commissars were abolished in the Red Army in 1924, only to be reinstituted following the German invasion; they were abolished again in 1942. The institution violated the concept of **one-man management,** which see.

military specialists (voenspetsy) Former tsarist officers who enlisted in Red Army service during the Civil War. They provided a great deal of continuity between the tsarist and Red armies, especially at the level of the general staff officers.

military tribunals Subordinate to the USSR Supreme Court, these are the special military courts within the armed forces.

militsiia The Soviet regular police.

Ministry of Internal Affairs (ministerstvo vnutrennikh del; MVD) In the paranoia of his latter years, Stalin created two secret police organs, the MVD and the Ministry of State Security (MGB).

Ministry of State Security (Ministerstvo gosudarstvennoi bezopasnosti; MGB) One of the two secret police organs created by Stalin in his later, demented years. The second was the Ministry of Internal Affairs (MVD). In 1953, the MVD absorbed the MGB.

minorities See **ethnic minorities.**

mir The council of the village commune under the tsars. The word also means "peace" and "world."

Moscow Patriarchate The office of the head of the Russian Orthodox church.

MPA See **Main Political Administration.**

MVD See **Ministry of Internal Affairs.**

narod The people.

Narodnaia volia See **People's Will.**

narodniki Populists. Pre-Marxist agrarian socialists who advocated salvation for Russia under a strong peasantry. The antecedents of the social revolutionaries.

Narodnoe khoziaistvo *Peoples' Economy*. The annual Soviet statistical handbook published since 1956.

narodnost Nationality. National character. Peopleness. The orientation of art and literature to mass needs and perceptions. See **socialist realism.**

national bourgeoisie Present or former Soviet citizens who stress national independence within the USSR. Also the Soviet description of entrepreneurs in the lesser developed countries.

national liberation movement See **wars of national liberation; world revolutionary forces.**

nationalism Although nationalism, along with religion, was rejected as an "opiate of the people," Stalin, faced with the German invasion during World War II, revived the concept under the label "Soviet patriotism."

nationalities problem A Western term pertaining to the difficulty of absorbing the national republics and their various cultures and languages into the union. See **ethnic minorities; sblizhenie; sliianie.**

NATO The North Atlantic Treaty Organization is a regional military organization of sixteen Western European and North American states designed to block Soviet expansionism in Europe. NATO members are Belgium, Canada, Denmark, the Federal Republic of Germany, France, Greece, Iceland, Italy, Luxembourg, the Netherlands, Norway, Portugal, Spain, Turkey, the United Kingdom, and the United States.

natural zones The eleven climatic, soil, and vegetation regions of the USSR stretching from the north to the south. They are arctic desert; subarctic tundra; forest tundra; taiga; mixed forest; broad-leaf forest; forest-steppe; steppe; semidesert; desert; and humid subtropic.

naturoplata See **payment in kind.**

Nazi–Soviet Pact The 1939 agreement between Germany and the USSR that included both a nonaggression agreement and a secret provision for the two powers to divide the Baltic states and Poland.

negation of the negation Synonymous with synthesis. Thus, it is the third moment in the dialectical process. In the dialectical process the thesis generates its opposite, the antithesis. The negation of the negation negates the negative aspects of both the thesis and the antithesis, preserves the positive elements, and raises them to a higher level.

nekulturnyi To be uncultured or crude.

neocolonialism Almost any activity in the developing nations undertaken by capitalist states (including aid) or capitalist business enterprises is considered neocolonialism. Although outright colonial takeover may not be the purpose, the Marxist-Leninist sees such activities as a means of foreign control, thus imperialist in nature.

NEP See **New Economic Policy.**

Nepmen Private traders who were active during the NEP period. See **New Economic Policy.**

new class In his book *The New Class,* the ousted Yugoslavian communist leader Milovan Djilas argued that Soviet party members had evolved into a new ruling class.

New Economic Policy (Novaia ekonomicheskaia politika; NEP) Lenin's abrupt shift in economic policy in 1921. By abandoning forced state requisitions of grain and reviving agricultural markets, Lenin succeeded in partially revitalizing agricultural production. Stalin's adoption of forced collectivization in 1928 ended the NEP.

new lands The vast grassland region of Kazakhstan and neighboring areas of the RSFSR that, until the time of Khrushchev, had never been plowed. However, in his search to solve the grain problem in the 1950s, Khrushchev caused some forty million hectares of those "virgin lands" to be plowed and sowed to grain.

New Rome A Western description of the Soviet desire that Moscow should be the capital of a communist world. It was derived from a perceived link between Russian messianism (and its idea of Orthodox Moscow as the Third Rome, or last and final capital of the Christian world before the second coming) and Soviet messianism.

new Soviet man The ideal Soviet person who is totally unselfish, marked by a Marxist-Leninist social consciousness, and thus totally devoted to "the collective." Assertedly, the basic outlook of such an individual is "what is mine is yours; what is yours is mine."

new Soviet nationalism See **nationalism.**

NKGB See **People's Commissariat of State Security.**

NKVD See **People's Commissariat of Internal Affairs.**

nomenklatura Appointments list. Also, individuals so favored as to be included on such a list. These lists, drawn up by higher party authorities, contain the names of individuals deemed eligible for important party and state posts. Thus, for example, the editor of *Pravda* is appointed by the Politburo from such a list.

non-chernozem Non-black-earth soil, especially the large agricultural zone in the northeast corner of the RSFSR.

nonparty active Eager citizens who, although they are not party members themselves, champion party programs and interests.

Nonproliferation Treaty A 1968 agreement among the nuclear powers, including the United States and the USSR, that prohibits the signatories from helping nonnuclear states to acquire nuclear weapons or the capability of producing such weapons.

norms Prescribed goals to be met by workers or enterprises if they perform satisfactorily. See **bonuses.**

NOT (Nauchnaia organizatsiia truda) Scientific Organization of Labor. A movement in the early 1920s that sought to blend Taylorism (the use of time and motion studies to increase worker output in factories) and socialist production to create greater rationality in the system of production. It is currently linked by Soviet systems analysts to the application of cybernetics, "the science of control," to the management of society.

Novoe vremia *New Times*. A Soviet journal.

Novosti A Soviet news agency.

Novyi mir *New World*. A leading literary journal.

NTS (Narodno-trudovoi soiuz) The National Labor Alliance or the Russian Solidarists. These are Soviet émigrés who, over the years, have worked in various ways against the USSR with the ultimate goal of overthrowing the regime.

obkom (oblastnoi komitet) The oblast party committee.

oblast A regional or territorial administrative subdivision of a republic. Sometimes such a region is referred to as a krai.

obligatory deliveries Especially as applicable to the collective farms, these are mandatory sales to the state by the enterprise, at state-set prices, of prescribed quantities of grain, milk, and other agricultural commodities.

oblispolkom (oblastnoi ispolnitelnyi komitet) The oblast soviet executive committee.

obshchestvennost The Soviet collective as a whole; the public or society.

obshchina Commune; now, generally, community. The peasant commune in prerevolutionary Russia carried with it the idea of collective ownership of the land and collective responsibilities to landlords and state. It is an attitude deeply rooted in Russian culture and history, but compatible with communist thought; it focuses attention on the group rather than the individual. See **collective; new Soviet man.**

October Manifesto Tsar Nicholas II's reply to the 1905 uprising, promising freedom of speech and assembly and voting rights as well as a representative legislature.

October Revolution The Bolsheviks' seizure of power on 25 October 1917 (Old Style). Now celebrated on 7 November. See **Julian calendar.**

Octobrists The prerevolutionary party of liberals, slightly to the left of center, who took their name from the 1905 October Manifesto and demanded the establishment of a constitutional system. See also **Little Octobrists.**

Ogonek *Little Light.* A major weekly pictorial magazine.

OGPU See **State Political Administration.**

Okhrana The tsarist secret police.

okrug See **autonomous territories.**

old calendar See **Julian calendar.**

on the conveyor This was a secret-police technique, commonplace during the Stalinist years, in which the accused was deprived of sleep and interrogated constantly by rotating teams of examiners with the object of exacting a confession of guilt from the accused.

one-man management (edinonachalie) Failing in early attempts to manage affairs through the collectives, a long-term Soviet practice has been to arrange enterprise management so that a key individual can be held responsible for successes and failures—for example, a plant manager or a state farm director.

openness (glasnost) The campaign led by Gorbachev to decrease secretiveness in the Soviet dialogue, especially calling for a more frank discussion of economic, political, and social problems. A demand that recurs in Russian public debate. For example, the cry for glasnost led to, among other reforms, a complete revision of the legal system under Alexander II. Also, in the early 1960s glasnost was one of the highest ideals of the literary dissenters.

"Operation Barbarossa" See **Barbarossa.**

opiate of the people According to Marxism-Leninism, emotional tools (namely, religion and nationalism) are used in the psychological manipulation of the masses by their capitalist masters, to make the exploited workers accept their fate.

orgburo (Organizatsionnoe biruo) Organization Bureau. Abolished in 1952, this was a subcommittee of the Central Committee of the CPSU, but subordinate to the Politburo.

Orthodox church See **Russian Orthodox church.**

otdel An office or department of a governmental ministry or of the central party apparatus.

otrezok (pl. **otrezki**) Land that was cut off from peasant allotments by the landlords at the time of the 1861 emancipation. Lenin issued a call for a return of the otrezki to the peasantry in a rather weak plank in the 1903 Party Congress. He was soon to learn that the peasants wanted more than just the otrezki—they wanted all the land.

otriady Detachments. See **link.**

"outcasts of Europe" A label applied to Germany and the USSR during the early post–World War I years because of their deviant behavior in international affairs. See **Rapallo Conference.**

palaces of culture Centers of art and entertainment for the Soviet masses.

Pan-Slavism A nationalistic aspiration for a union of all Slavic peoples.

parasitism Able-bodied, jobless individuals deemed not to be making a positive contribution to the economy and society are seen to be engaging in parasitism.

Partiinaia zhizn *Party Life.* A party journal concerned largely with party affairs.

partiinost Party mindedness, party spirit. Placing party interests above all else. See **socialist realism.**

partorg (partiinyi organizator) A party organizer employed mostly at the primary level of the party. The partorg's goals are to stimulate the growth of party organization and to strengthen the loyalty of party members to the regime. Partorgs at the primary level of the party generally work full time on party affairs; their counterparts in larger organizations do not.

party card An official membership card issued to every member of the party. Periodically, in a card exchange designed to weed out the dead wood, new cards are issued to only those members who pass a favorable review. Card no. 1 is always reserved for Lenin, and no. 2 for the individual who is the general secretary.

party cell See **primary party organization.**

Party Commission An apparatus of the Central Committee that enforces party discipline and examines appeals from members of local party units who have been expelled or otherwise penalized.

party congresses See **Congress of the CPSU.**

party discipline Particularly as dictated by the doctrine of democratic centralism, all party members are held strictly to promoting the party line at all times and without deviation.

party plenum A special party meeting. Thus a plenum of the CC CPSU is a special meeting of the Central Committee between party congresses.

party program An outline of party goals adopted during a party congress. The CPSU has had four party programs during its existence; the latest was adopted by the Twenty-seventh Party Congress in February 1986.

party rules Guidelines for party members adopted during a party congress.

party schools A network of special schools designed to train citizens (especially party members) in Marxism-Leninism and leadership and management. The "higher party schools" concentrate on training the future top elite.

party secretary At all levels there are party executive committees (for example, the Politburo, raikom, and so on) led by a party secretary. Thus, the most powerful individual in the USSR is the first secretary of the CC CPSU, who usually takes the title "General Secretary" to designate his supreme position. Collectively, the party secretaries are the several thousand most powerful individuals who run the USSR.

patriarch of Moscow The head of the Russian Orthodox church.

payment in kind (Naturoplata) Payment to a collective farm peasant in the form of a portion of the farm's produce, especially fodder for the peasant's private livestock.

"peace, land, and bread" Lenin's major slogan upon his return to Petrograd in April 1917.

peaceful coexistence A relationship with capitalist nations that excludes war between capitalist and socialist states and applauds peaceful economic competition but assumes the eventual collapse of capitalism. Therefore, it encourages friction and strife within and among capitalist countries by every means, short of all-out war. A "relaxation of tensions" is a Soviet synonym for "détente." Small wars of national liberation in underdeveloped nations are to be encouraged and supported actively, provided that support does not provoke a major conflict with the strongholds of capitalism. Assertedly, the idea originated with Lenin; thus "Leninist peaceful coexistence." See **inevitability of war doctrine.**

peasant The Soviet farmer. Although the view is not officially sanctioned, the peasants are generally considered to be on the bottom rung of society, especially in terms of education and class consciousness. See **semiproletarian.**

peasant emancipation By order to Tsar Alexander II, the serfs received their personal freedom in 1861. Although those who were associated with the land received parcels of land with which they could presumably support themselves, the parcels were insufficient and were saddled with very high redemption payments.

people's assessors See **assessors.**

People's Commissariat of Internal Affairs (Narodnyi Komissariat Vnutrennikh Del, NKVD) Soviet secret police. In 1934 the GPU was renamed the NKVD and later, the Ministry of Internal Affairs (MVD).

People's Commissariat of State Security (Narodnyi Komissariat Gosudarstvennoi Bezopasnosti, NKGB) Later, the Minister of State Security (MGB) and presently Committee for State Security (KGB). Soviet secret police.

people's courts Local courts. The lowest level of courts in the Soviet judicial hierarchy. They consist of a judge and two lay assessors.

people's democracy A form of "proletarian dictatorship" created in Eastern Europe and the developing nations that accepts Marxism-Leninism and follows to a satisfactory degree the Soviet model.

people's inspectorates Ordinary citizens charged with checking the books and inventories of an enterprise and reporting their findings to higher authorities. Although usually workers in the enterprise they monitor, the inspectors are not supposed to be close relatives of the enterprise's top administrators.

People's Will (Narodnaia volia) A populist revolutionary group committed to assassinating leading government figures. Lenin's older brother Alexander, who was hanged in May 1887 for an attempt on Tsar Alexander III's life, was a member.

perestroika See **restructuring.**

permafrost Land in the northern latitudes that remains permanently frozen, even in the warmest summers. Roughly the northern third of the Soviet landmass is composed of permafrost.

permanent revolution A doctrine particularly championed by Trotsky that the party should give priority to constantly furthering the world revolution.

personality cult See **cult of personality.**

Pioneer palaces Places of culture, entertainment, and recreation for Soviet youth.

Pioneers See **Young Pioneers.**

Pionerskaya pravda The Young Pioneers' journal.

planned economy Western specialists often refer to the USSR and the other states that reject market mechanisms for central planning in economic guidance as "planned economies."

planning Central planning is a vital part of the Soviet system, especially in the economic realm. Rejecting marketplace mechanisms, Soviet leaders attempt to plan all activities. Thus for the workers, managers, and high government administrators, achievement of plan goals is a prime measure of success or failure. See **five-year plan; gosplan; planned economy.**

plenum CC CPSU meetings between the party congresses. See **party plenum.**

Politburo (Politicheskoe biuro) The Political Bureau is the executive committee of the Central Committee CPSU, and the center of Soviet power, led by the general secretary (for example, Khrushchev, Brezhnev, or Gorbachev). First created in 1917, the Politburo has varied in size, but usually it consists of some dozen full, voting members plus a smaller number of candidate members. The name was changed to Presidium in 1952, but the term Politburo was restored in 1966.

political crimes According to Soviet law these are "particularly dangerous crimes against the state." Thus they are acts that could damage the system. Examples would be publishing material critical of the party or the system or the names of KGB officials who are not part of the public record.

political officer Party members of the military attached at various levels of command and responsible for party affairs. The **zampolit** and, at the lower levels, the **politruk,** both of which see. Ultimately they report to the Main Political Administration.

politruk (politicheskii rukovoditel) Political instructor or political commissar. Formerly, party members within the Red Army who provided political education and propaganda among troops at the company level, and who served as political watchdogs on military commanders. The politruk existed during the Civil War but was abolished in 1924. The office was revived in 1941 but abolished again in 1942. Existence of the politruk violated the principle of "one-man management" but provided for more effective party control. See **political officer.**

polycentrism A Western term used to describe the differences between Moscow and other Marxist-Leninist states over policies, practices, and doctrines—especially since the 1956 Hungarian uprising. The rise of the term signaled the end of the previous widely held view that there were no serious differences among the world's Marxist-Leninist leaders. See **Eurocommunism.**

pood A Russian measure of weight equal to 36.113 pounds.

popular front(s) With the rise of fascism and the Spanish Civil War, during the 1930s, communist parties were encouraged to cooperate with willing noncommunist political groups. The fronts were key to Soviet penetration of Eastern Europe during World War II. Also see **united front.**

populists See **narodniki; People's Will.**

Potemkin village Fake villages that Prince Grigorii Potemkin, advisor to Catherine the Great, built to make the countryside seem more populated than it was.

Potsdam Conference The summit, held from 17 July to 2 August 1945, in which agreements were made among the Allies on postwar Germany. Truman, Stalin, and Churchill (later replaced by Attlee) attended.

PPO See **primary party organization.**

Prague Spring See **Czech Spring.**

Pravda *Truth.* The leading party newspaper.

pravo kontrolia See **right of control.**

prefect See **party secretary.**

president The chairman of the Presidium of the Supreme Soviet. The official, ceremonial head of the Soviet state.

presidium An executive committee. Between 1952 and 1966 the Politburo was known as the Presidium of the CC CPSU. See **Presidium of the Supreme Soviet.**

Presidium of the Supreme Soviet An executive committee of the Supreme Soviet serving primarily as the chief legislative body between sessions of the Supreme Soviet. The chairman is the official head of the Soviet state, thus a rough equivalent of a Western president. However, the president is not as powerful as the general secretary of the party.

primary party organization The basic primary unit of the party. All party members belong to such a unit. Until 1934 they were known as communist party cells and, outside the USSR, were kept secret.

private plots Small household gardens (an acre or less) of state land allotted to most peasants and some urban residents. The plots account for a disproportionate amount of Soviet food, especially fruits and vegetables.

procuracy (prokuratura) The hierarchy of Soviet state prosecuting attorneys found at all administrative levels.

procurator general The chief Soviet state prosecutor has much more power than his U.S. counterpart, although the procurator is somewhat similar to the U.S. attorney general.

procurement price In agriculture, the price paid by the Soviet government to collectives for the legally required delivery of food and raw materials to the state.

profilaktorii Special institution for the treatment of alcoholics and drug users.

profsoiuz See **trade unions.**

proletarian See **proletariat.**

proletarian internationalism See **internationalism.**

proletariat According to Marxism, the exploited workers' class in capitalist society.

proletcult (proletarskaia kultura) Proletarian culture. An avant-garde Marxist movement in the arts in the post-1917 period. Led by A. A. Bogdanov and supported by some Bolshevik intellectuals, the movement got very little sympathy from Lenin and was suppressed.

propaganda Selected information and admonishments directed at the masses to train them in Marxist theory and to direct them toward Soviet goals. In the USSR the term "propaganda" does not have negative connotations. Indeed, it is an integral part of the communications media and the educational system to effect mass mobilization. See **agitprop.**

propaganda department See **agitprop.**

protektsiia Protectionism, patronage, influence as applied to the leadership system. See **nomenklatura.**

province An administrative region. Thus, either a krai or an oblast.

Provisional Government From the time of the abdication of the tsar in March until the November Bolshevik coup d'état (October, Julian calendar) Russia was ruled first by a group headed by Price Lvov and, after July, by Alexander Kerensky.

purge trials The trials in the 1930s resulting in the imprisonment or execution of the vast majority of Stalin's real or imagined opposition.

purges Periodic ejection by the party of unwanted members in order to purify its ranks.

quintal See **centner.**

rabfak (rabochii fakultet) Workers' school. In early years, the workers' faculty provided elementary schooling for adult workers. Khrushchev was enrolled in one in 1918, which set him on his way toward the party inner circle.

rabselkor (raboche-selskii korrespondent) Worker-peasant correspondent. The use and encouragement of peasant and worker comment and criticism (usually in the form of letters) by the Soviet press. This process serves to link the masses with party goals and to give the people a sense of participation.

raiispolkom (raionnyi ispolnitelnyi komitet) The executive committee of a district soviet.

raikom (raionnyi komitet) A district party committee.

raion A subdivision of a krai or an oblast. A district. A rural administrative unit roughly the size of a large U.S. county.

raion agro-industrial associations The RAPO. See **agro-industrial district union.**

raion inspectorate See **inspector organizers.**

raivoenkomat (raionnyi voennyi komissariat) The district military enlistment and registration office that also reviews the recruits' political records.

Rapallo Conference During the 1922 Genoa Conference, German and Russian diplomats met in the nearby town of Rapallo, an action that reestablished relations between the two outcasts of Europe.

rapo See **agro-industrial district union.**

raskulachivanie See **dekulakization; kulak.**

rayon See **raion.**

recoupment period The period of time necessary to recover a given investment. Some Soviet economists have proposed the use of their interpretation of the recoupment period to decide among various investment alternatives. For practical reasons, however, monetary savings rather than savings in hours of labor-time are usually used to compute the recoupment period.

Red Army A name applied to the Bolshevik army fashioned by Trotsky in 1918 to combat the counterrevolutionary White forces. It was renamed the Soviet Army in 1946.

Red Guard Armed factory workers (mostly) who, as a unit, participated in the 1917 Bolshevik coup d'état.

Red Square (Krasnaia ploshchad) The large open area outside the Kremlin in which major parades and celebrations are held. In it is St. Basil's Cathedral, and along its edge are Lenin's Tomb and the Kremlin wall, in which Soviet dignitaries are buried.

Red Star See ***Krasnaia zvezda.***

redemption payments Although the peasant emancipation of 1861 politically freed the serfs, what little land they received was saddled with impossibly high redemption payments, which became the source of much unrest in rural Russia.

reformism Improving society by change through the existing political structure, not by changing the structure itself. According to Marxism-Leninism, it is an attempt to improve society by changing the existing socioeconomic and political structures without dealing with the existing contradictions, and under capitalism it is doomed to failure. Reformism is an attempt by a ruling class to postpone the inevitable revolution and triumph of the working class.

religion Although religious belief is not outlawed in the USSR, churches and religious practices are both seriously discouraged and curtailed. See **atheism.**

repair and technical service stations The RTS. They succeeded the MTS in 1958, but they did not control the equipment as did the MTS. They were more a repair service, a parts distributor, and a supply depot for new agricultural equipment. The RTS were abolished in 1961 in favor of the All-Union Farm Machinery Association.

republics The fifteen major administrative subdivisions in the USSR, each based upon the largest native ethnic group in the area.

restructuring (perestroika) Gorbachev's campaign to revitalize the party, society, and economy by means of adjustments of socioeconomic and political mechanisms.

revision commissions Groups of collective farm workers charged with serving as watchdogs over financial activities, including auditing the books. Personnel on this body are not supposed to be close relatives of the members of the farm administration.

revisionism Attempt to change Marxist-Leninist doctrine. One of the cardinal sins of communism is to alter the "science of Marxism-Leninism." Thus, doctrinal changes proclaimed by Mao Zedong and Tito resulted in significant Soviet hostility.

Revolution, the The 7 November 1917 Bolshevik seizure of power in Petrograd. Also, all of the factors and forces working together that Marxist-Leninists believe will lead eventually to world communism.

"revolution from above" Although Soviet officials never have admitted that force was used in the collectivization of the farms in the 1930s, Stalin did refer to the action as a "revolution from above"—that is, a Moscow-directed campaign.

revolution of national liberation See **wars of national liberation.**

revolutionary bourgeoisie According to Marxism-Leninism, members of the capitalist class in the colonies who side with the struggle to oust imperialist control.

revolutionary socialists Individuals of socialist persuasion in capitalist nations who agree that force is required to overthrow the existing system.

right of control The party claim to the right to control all aspects of Soviet affairs. Strictly speaking, the party claim is the right of "verification," that is, the right to check on management and other state activities.

RSFSR See **Russian Soviet Federated Socialist Republic.**

RTS See **repair and technical service stations.**

ruble The Soviet monetary unit, equal to 100 kopecks. Soviet officials prohibit the use of rubles in international exchange. In recent years visitors to the USSR have been charged some $1.40 per ruble. Although the real value of a ruble is difficult to ascertain, many would argue that an exchange rate of two rubles to a dollar would be closer to reality.

Russian empire The people and territory governed under the tsars prior to 1917.

Russian Orthodox church The official state church under the tsars. Today the largest single religious group in the USSR is the Russian Orthodox church. It is linked with other Orthodox churches such as the Greek Orthodox church and the Orthodox church in America.

Russian Social Democratic Labor Party See **social democrats.**

Russian Soviet Federated Socialist Republic The Russian Republic that is the largest of the fifteen Soviet Socialist Republics.

Russification A Western claim that in encouraging the universal use of the Russian language and, particularly, the suppression of religious and cultural beliefs and practices of minority nationalities, there is a Soviet policy of transforming all the USSR's national peoples into cultural Russians.

rynok Market. See **kolkhoz market.**

SALT I The Strategic Arms Limitation Talks, initiated in Helsinki in 1969. SALT I was ratified by both the United States and the USSR. It limited ABM (antiballistic missile) systems as well as the number of missile-delivery systems with nuclear warheads.

SALT II A comprehensive U.S.–USSR accord on strategic arms limitations signed by both parties in 1979, but not ratified by the U.S. Senate. It placed numerical ceilings of

820 on multiple-warhead ICBMs, of 1,200 on multiple-warhead ICBMs and submarine-launched ballistic missiles, and of 1,320 for a combination of multiple warhead missiles and bombers with air-launched cruise missiles.

samizdat Self-publication. The unofficial publication and duplication of manuscripts by copying stories, poems, plays, articles, novels, and even nonfiction works. This often involves retyping entire manuscripts by readers. The practice was particularly stimulated in the 1960s by the fear of the restoration of Stalin's image.

samogon Home-distilled vodka, moonshine. Illegally distilled alcoholic beverages.

samokritika See **criticism and self-criticism.**

satellite states A Western term for the Eastern European states closely tied economically, politically, and militarily to the USSR.

sblizhenie Coming together or rapprochement, as applied to the short-term differences among the Soviet nationalities. Used in reference to current nationality policy in the USSR, it stresses the acceptance of Marxist-Leninist norms in the pursuit of political and economic modernization. See, in contrast, **sliianie.** Also see **ethnic minorities; nationalities problem; Russification.**

school of the long day (shkola prodlennogo dnia) Extended-day school. Although formal classwork ends early in the afternoon, most schools keep the children at other tasks until late in the day. This is because in the vast majority of families, both parents work. Thus, if the children were released earlier, they would be returning to empty homes.

science of society The conviction that Marxism-Leninism provides laws that govern society and behavior that are just as scientific as the laws of natural science. Thus, communism is the only correct form of society.

scientific communism See **science of society.**

scissors crisis The crisis that developed during the NEP in the 1920s because consumer goods were scarce and expensive, and the peasants were hoarding their grain rather than selling it. Industrial development demanded the sale of the grain at low prices in order to feed the cities, pay for imports, and produce consumer goods for which the peasants would spend money. The dilemma produced a stalemate resolved only by Stalin's "emergency measures" of 1929 against the peasants and especially the kulaks. The description was originated by Trotsky who observed that on a chart the reversal that had occurred in the "terms of trade" between the products of the town and those of the country was similar to the opening blades of a pair of scissors.

Second Great Imperialist War, the The Soviet name for World War II, also known as "The Great Patriotic War." According to Marxist-Leninist theory, all modern wars stem from the inevitability of capitalist imperialism.

Second International An association of communist parties founded in 1889 that collapsed with the onset of World War I.

secret speech In 1956, behind the closed doors of the Twentieth Party Congress, Khrushchev spoke of the excesses of Stalin, especially his crimes against party members.

Secretariat An organ of the party Central Committee that is responsible for overseeing the fulfillment of party policy.

secretary At all levels of the party hierarchy, the secretaries are the individuals in key leadership roles. The first secretary of a raion is the most powerful person in that district. Thus, the general secretary of the CC CPSU (Khrushchev, Brezhnev, or Gorbachev) is the most powerful individual in the USSR.

seksot (sekrentnyi sotrudnik) An informer who reports the activities of his comrades to the secret police.

selkhoztekhnika An agency responsible for agricultural supplies.

selsovet (Selskii sovet) The village soviet.

semiproletarian Whereas previous Marxist writings had not credited the peasantry with a class consciousness that would include them on the side of the revolutionary movement, Lenin argued that the landless and exploited peasants shared, in part, a class consciousness similar to that of the proletariat.

serfdom Until they were officially emancipated in 1861, the vast majority of the peasants in the Russian empire were the property of landlords.

seven-year plan Near the end of the Sixth Five-Year Plan period, the plan was abandoned, probably because of the impossibility of fulfilling it, and replaced by a seven-year plan for the 1959–65 period. Subsequently, however, the Soviets have returned to five-year planning periods.

shabashnik An individual who supplies services or repairs on the side for private gain.

Shakhty prosecutions A trial held in the city of Shakhty in 1928 for a number of engineers accused of deliberately "wrecking" production. This was the beginning of a wave of terror directed against the technical intelligentsia.

sheftsvo Patronage or sponsorship used to advance an individual's career.

shock-workers' movement Prior to the Stakanovite movement, this was a campaign among workers intended to increase their productivity. See **Stakhanovism.**

Siberia An imprecise term that refers roughly to the vast eastern regions of the USSR, especially the territory between the Ural Mountains and the Pacific Ocean.

Siberian Division of the Academy of Sciences Akademogorodok.

Slavophiles Russian intellectuals of the mid-nineteenth century who sought to create a conservative utopia on the basis of old-Russian custom and tradition. They believed that Russian nationality had been corrupted by Western ideas and sought a purity in the distant past and in the Orthodox faith. See **Westernizers.**

sliivanie Merging, as applied to a long-term way of ending differences among Soviet nationalities.

slogans Party-proclaimed phrases and resolutions that are a key part of the propaganda effort. On May Day and other special occasions new slogans appear. They are displayed constantly on signs and posters throughout the USSR.

Smersh (smert shpionam) "Death to the spies." A special security unit during World War II assigned to eliminate all real and potential enemies within the USSR.

SNK See **Sovnarkom.**

sobornost Consiliarism. Identification with a larger social entity for the common good. Rooted in the traditional Russian sense of community, today the term implies Soviet solidarity. See **collective.**

social democrats Arising in Russia as underground Marxist groups in the 1870s, this movement evolved into the Russian Social Democratic Labor Party which, in 1903, split into the Bolsheviks and Mensheviks.

social revolutionaries The SRs. Founded in Russia in 1902 by Marxist descendants of the populists, this was a peasant-oriented party.

socialism Public ownership of, essentially, all means of production. According to Lenin, socialism is an intermediate stage between the dictatorship of the proletariat and full communism. Often, rather than use the term "communist" to describe the USSR, the leaders will use the term "socialist." See **advanced socialism.**

socialism in one country Prior to Stalin's rule, party doctrine maintained that communism (that is, full socialism) could be achieved only on a worldwide scale. However, with Stalin's 1936 pronouncement that the USSR was building socialism, a shift in the doctrine occurred.

socialist commonwealth Marxist-Leninist countries that align themselves with Moscow, especially on foreign-policy matters.

socialist competition (sotsialesticheskoe sorevnovanie) Also referred to as "collective competition." Competition of a special, cooperative kind, such as that presumably staged in the USSR between and among working groups, factories, and farms to encourage greater production and/or output per worker.

socialist consciousness The mind set of individuals whose views reflect Marxist-Leninist values, particularly as articulated by the party leadership.

socialist construction A concept resulting from the view that the revolution envisioned by Marx and Engels has now assumed a worldwide character. Every communist system will have to be made fit for the machine age after its emergence on the world scene even though it will require sacrifice and some alienation.

socialist democracy See **democracy.**

socialist discipline Strict adherence by individuals and groups to the dictates of the Marxist-Leninist laws of society.

socialist emulation Following the correct Marxist-Leninist path in all things. See **socialist competition; socialist discipline.**

socialist order Arranging all things in the correct socialist way.

socialist realism In art and literature the ultimate measure of quality is whether a work contributes to the building of socialism among the masses. According to the doctrine, literature is to be "realist in form and socialist in content." This was particularly promoted by Zhdanov, Stalin's friend and fellow Politburo member, as a major tool for mass indoctrination (thus Zhdanovism). Three key principles of Soviet aesthetics have been identified: klassovost (classness or class mindedness), narodnost (national mindedness) and partiinost (party mindedness).

socialist revolutionaries See **social revolutionaries.**

socialist work ethic An attitude towards work that places the goals of the collective and the state above all else.

Solidarity (Solidarnost; in Polish, solidarnosc) A mass, noncommunist, trade-union movement among Poles calling for political and economic reforms and an end to party domination. It is strongly opposed by Soviet leaders. The name is obviously an intentional ironic play on the communist term *trudiashchukhsia solidarnost,* "international solidarity of the toiling masses," a presumed emotional unity among workers of the world (note the line in the Internationale, the communist anthem, "solidarity forever!"). Beginning in Poland in 1980 as a workers' movement, Solidarnosc found wide support among all strata of society and forged close links with the Catholic church. In 1981, when it called for a nonparty government and free elections, the Solidarity movement was suppressed by the Polish regime.

sovet See **soviet.**

soviet (sovet) Council. An adjective denoting "of the USSR" just as "American" can denote "of the United States." The term originated with the forming of workers' soviets during the 1905 revolution. The term is used at all levels of the governmental hierarchy—for example, republic soviet, local soviet, etc.

Soviet of Nationalities One of the two houses of the Supreme Soviet, "elected" on the basis of representation (at least minimal) of all of the important ethnic groups in the USSR, which are organized as republics, autonomous oblasts, or autonomous territories.

Soviet of the Union One of the two houses of the Supreme Soviet, "elected" on the basis of equal representation of all the population.

Soviet nationalism From a non-Soviet point of view, an attitude that evolved during World War II that enmeshed traditional Russian nationalism with Soviet Marxism-Leninism.

Soviet patriotism A meld of belief in Marxism-Leninism and a love of things Soviet. Under Stalin, members of the Comintern were expected to give their first loyalty to the Soviet Union, the birthplace and bastion of socialism.

Sovietology A Western term designating the systematic study of Russian and Soviet history, Soviet economics and society, and, indeed, anything that helps expand knowledge and understanding of the USSR.

sovkhov See **state farm.**

sovnarkhoz (sovet narodnogo khoziaistva) The economic council. Also, for a time, Khrushchev worked to establish the sovnarkhozy as a new form of regional economic administration for the whole of the USSR.

Sovnarkom (Sovet narodnykh komissarov) The SNK. Council of Peoples' Commissars. Prior to 1946 what is now known as the Council of Ministers of the Supreme Soviet was called the Sovnarkom.

sputnik The Russian word for satellite or fellow traveler, thus a space satellite. Also, the name of the official youth travel agency.

SRs See **social revolutionaries.**

Stakhanovism In 1935 A. G. Stakhanov, a coal miner, so arranged the work that he and the colleagues on his shift were able to set new output records. (There is some suspicion that the effort may have been rigged.) For some time Stakhanovite activities were promoted. However, because they tended to glorify the individual at the expense of the collective, Stakhanovism fell from favor. Now group competitions are emphasized. See **socialist competition.**

Stalin Constitution The constitution promulgated in 1936, and since supplanted by a 1977 document. See **Constitution.**

Stalin Prize See **Lenin Prize.**

Stalinism The institutions and practices, especially mass terror, associated with Stalin's long period of rule.

starosta The village elder in tsarist Russia.

State Defense Committee (Gosudarstvennyi komitet oborony; GKO) Created in June 1941 to coordinate the entire Soviet defense effort under Stalin's leadership, this committee provided the central link between state, party, and military organizations.

state farm (sovetskoe khoziaistvo; sovkhoz) In contrast to the collective farms (kolkhozy), which ostensibly are cooperatives, the sovkhozy are state-managed enterprises and the workers are salaried state employees.

State Political Administration (Gosudarstvennoe politicheskoe upravlenie; GPU) This security service was created in 1922 to replace the Cheka, and later became the OGPU (Obedinennoe gosudarstvennoe politicheskoe upravlenie).

Stavka Headquarters of the Soviet Supreme High Command during World War II.

steppe the vast prairie grasslands.

Stevenson amendment Legislation in the U.S. Senate in the mid-1970s that sharply restricted the amount of money the Soviet Union could borrow from the United States. See **Helsinki Accords; Jackson–Vanik amendment.**

stiliaga A style-conscious youth given to uncritical display of fashion in clothing and behavior. Comparable to the U.S. "zoot suiter" of the 1940s or the more recent British "punk."

Stolypin reforms Russian prime minister Peter Stolypin attempted to solve the peasant problem with agrarian reforms that promoted a strong yeoman peasantry. He was assassinated in 1911.

storming (shturnovshchina) Rushed work or production spurt. Often, near the end of the month, Soviet enterprise managers discover that they are lagging behind plan goals. As a result, feverish efforts, including overtime for the workers, are implemented in an effort to meet plan.

Strategic Arms Limitation Talks See **SALT I; SALT II.**

stukach Informer, stool pigeon. Slang for a Soviet citizen who has been recruited to report on the activities and comments of fellow workers or residents.

subbotnik Saturday worker, or a voluntary, unpaid worker. Once a year in April, to commemorate Lenin's birthday, many Soviet workers return to their jobs on a designated Saturday and put in an extra day's labor for the state without pay.

sukhovei A hot, desiccating wind that arises in the southern regions of the USSR and can be very damaging to crops.

superstructure and base The Marxist doctrine that all socioeconomic relations are determined by people's relationship to the means of production (the base). Thus, the form of government, indeed, all institutions (the superstructure), flow from the base.

Supreme Court The highest court in the Soviet judicial hierarchy. Although the court serves as the last court of appeal and will help interpret laws, it does not practice judicial review.

Supreme Soviet The Soviet parliament. A legislative body comprised of two houses, the Soviet of Nationalities and the Soviet of the Union.

surplus value A Marxian doctrine that the value added to commodities by workers under capitalism is the source of profits that the capitalist owners steal from the workers.

taiga The vast northern region of the USSR covered by coniferous forests.

talmud The collection of writings that constitute Jewish civil law. In the USSR the term is also applied to the list of information banned from publication. See **index.**

tamizdat Illegal underground literature smuggled into the USSR from outside its borders.

TASS (Telegrafnoe agenstvo sovetskogo soiuza) The Telegraph Agency of the Soviet Union, an official news agency.

taxes Although there are direct Soviet taxes, and an income tax, they are all very low, allowing the claim that many services and benefits in the USSR are free. However, because the vast majority of the state's revenues comes from selling state-produced commodities in state stores, the citizens are, in fact, very heavily taxed by a hidden, indirect turnover tax.

technikum An institution devoted to technical training. Technical college.

territorial production administrations The TPAs. Local administrative subdivisions created on the "territorial production principle." Each of the some fifteen hundred TPAs was responsible for some forty kolkhozy and sovkhozy.

The TPAs were one of Khrushchev's administrative reforms that were later abandoned.

thaw, the A term used to describe the relatively relaxed atmosphere after the death of Stalin that resulted in the release of millions of political prisoners and a relaxation of literary censorship.

Third International See **Comintern.**

Third Rome See **New Rome.**

Titoism The brand of Marxist-Leninist deviationism practiced by the Yugoslavian leader Tito, especially his emphasis on nationalism.

tolkach A pusher or facilitator. An individual within an economic enterprise who serves to further its success by employing blat (pull), largely by making extralegal agreements and deals.

totalitarianism Extreme authoritarian rule, especially marked by the use of mass terror for popular control. See **Stalinism.**

tovarishch Comrade. A traditional Russian term for companion.

TOZ (Tovarishchestvo po sovmestnoi obrabotke zemli) Society for the Joint Cultivation of Land. The least collectivized and most informal system of organizing agriculture between 1917 and 1930. It was a loose cooperative in which some pastures were held, and marketing was done, in common.

TPA See **territorial production administrations.**

trade unions Soviet workers' organizations based upon enterprises. Virtually all eligible workers are members of these unions because they manage such important matters as housing, worker benefits, and complaints. Strikes are illegal in the Soviet Union.

Trans-Siberian Railroad The rail "land bridge" that links Western Europe with the Soviet Far East, Japan, and Korea.

trickle-down theory A Leninist doctrine that nineteenth-century imperialism was so profitable that it allowed the colonial states to pass on some of the overseas booty to the workers as a bribe. Thus, the largess was allowed to "trickle down" to the workers, especially their leaders.

troika A vehicle drawn by three horses. Also, a team of three individuals, such as the Stalin–Bukharin–Rykov leadership in 1925.

Trotskyism The leftist view championed by Trotsky during his contest with Stalin for Lenin's mantle and especially his stress on furthering world revolution rather than on building the Soviet state.

Trotskyite Anyone accused of the leftist deviationism associated with Trotsky.

trud *Labor.* The Soviet trade union newspaper.

trudoden See **labor day.**

Truman Doctrine A 1947 declaration by President Truman that further Soviet territorial expansion must be resisted.

TsK (tsentralnyi komitet) A central committee.

tundra Treeless plains. The vast Arctic and northern Siberian regions of the USSR.

turnover tax See **taxes.**

udarnik An industrial shock worker. In the early years, these workers broke records and were given honors and social benefits such as food, housing, and consumer goods. This action broke with the egalitarianism theretofore espoused. Featured as new heroes of the socialist society, they were sent by the thousands to participate in collectivization of agriculture, to help liquidate the kulaks, and to staff the kolkhozy and MTS.

ukaz Ukase. A decree issued by the Presidium of the Supreme Soviet. Also, any governmental edict.

underemployment Although officially all eligible able-bodied workers in the USSR have employment, most Western analysts agree that there is vast underemployment in the USSR, particularly as measured by the low rates of labor productivity when compared with those of most other industrial states.

"unholy alliance" The *Times* (London) description of the German–Soviet Berlin Treaty of 1926.

Union of Soviet Composers; Composers' Union All individuals in the USSR who earn their living as composers must belong to this party-dominated organization if they expect to have their material published. See **creative unions.**

Union of Soviet Socialist Republics As proclaimed in 1922, this is the official name of the Soviet Union.

Union of Soviet Writers; Writers' Union All individuals in the USSR who earn their living as writers must belong to this party-dominated organization if they expect to have their material published. That reality alone, more than direct censorship, undoubtedly is the major means of control over the Soviet press. See **creative unions.**

union republic ministries Ministries of the USSR that have counterpart ministries in each of the republics. For example, there are both a Ministry of Agriculture in Moscow and a counterpart Ukrainian Ministry of Agriculture in Kiev.

united front A Soviet policy that arose in the 1930s to encourage cooperation between communist parties and moderate socialists against right-wing authoritarianism. Also see **popular front(s).**

USSR See **Union of Soviet Socialist Republics.**

vanguard of the proletariat The Communist Party. Claiming that the party has the responsibility of leading the workers, Lenin declared that it is the "vanguard of the proletariat." See **right of control.**

Viliams system See **Williams system.**

virgin land campaign See **new lands.**

voluntary militia The druzhini. Ordinary citizens who, often wearing red arm bands, assist the regular police.

Voprosy filosofii *Questions of Philosophy.* The major Soviet philosophical journal.

vozhd Leader. Stalin was often referred to as "Vozhd."

Vremia "Time." The major national evening TV news program originating in Moscow.

VTUZ (vysshee tekhnicheskoe uchebnoe zavedenie) An institution for higher technical education.

VUZ (vysshee uchebnoe zavedenie) An institution of higher learning.

War Communism The draconian economic policy followed during the 1918–21 Civil War period, including the forced requisitioning of the peasants' grain.

wars of national liberation Any armed uprising that serves to weaken the "imperialists'" grip on the Third World.

Warsaw Pact The Warsaw Treaty Organization (WTO) is a military alliance between the USSR and its Eastern European client states that was formed in 1955. In part the creation of the pact was in response to the inclusion of West Germany in NATO. Warsaw Pact members are Albania, Bulgaria, Czechoslovakia, the German Democratic Republic, Hungary, Poland, Romania, and the USSR. In 1962, Albania was no longer invited to Warsaw Pact meetings, although it was not formally expelled.

Warsaw Treaty Organization See **Warsaw Pact.**

wedding palaces Buildings designated for weddings in which Soviet authorities perform such ceremonies. Although many couples are married also by the clergy, church weddings are not officially recognized.

Westernizers Russian liberals of the mid-nineteenth century who believed that further progress in Russia would come with the development of Western institutions. See, in contrast, **Slavophiles.**

White Army Although the various leaders often disagreed violently, the Russian-based military groups that fought against the Bolsheviks during the 1918–21 Civil War were collectively known as the White Army.

Williams System Also, *Viliams system.* A universal grass-crop rotation system advocated by agricultural biologist and soil specialist Vasilii R. Viliams (of American parentage). Implemented by Stalin, the system probably did more harm than good to Soviet agriculture.

world revolution The Marxist-Leninist doctrine that ongoing fundamental changes will ultimately culminate in total world communism.

world revolutionary forces A Soviet doctrine that the three major factors working toward the "World Revolution" are "the world system of socialism" (with Moscow recognized as its headquarters); the "international workers' movement"; and "the national liberation movement."

world system of socialism The Soviet view that there is a commonwealth of advanced socialist states that have adopted the Soviet state model and that accept Moscow's interpretation of Marxism-Leninism. See **world revolutionary forces.**

Writers' Union See **Union of Soviet Writers.**

xenophobia Fear of foreigners. Many Western analysts believe that the repeated invasions of tsarist Russia and the

Soviet Union have engendered a widespread Russian and Soviet fear of foreigners.

Yalta Conference A February 1945 summit meeting of Churchill, Roosevelt, and Stalin concerning the status of Eastern Europe and the Far East.

YCL See **Young Communist League.**

Yezhovshchina The extreme terror practiced in 1937 and 1938, led by Nikolai Yezhov, then the head of the secret police.

Young Communist League (YCL; Komsomol; Kommunisticheskii soiuz molodezhi) The party-sponsored organization for young people generally from fifteen to twenty-five years of age, and a training ground for future party members.

Young Marx The term used to describe the writings of Marx before the issuance of the *Communist Manifesto* in 1848. In that earlier period his major stress was on humanism rather than economics.

Young Pioneers The junior affiliate of the Young Communist League. Composed of youth ten to sixteen years of age, it is comparable to the Boy and Girl Scouts. Though most of the activities concentrate on sports and hobbies, the behavior of the members is supposed to serve as an "example to all children." Leaders are usually members of the Young Communist League.

zagotzerno A grain collection point.

zakon A government statute or law.

zampolit (Zamestitel komandira po politicheskoe chasti) See **Main Political Administration; political officer.**

Zhdanovism; zhdanovshchina See **socialist realism.**

Zhurnalist The journalists' trade magazine.

Zil (Zavod imeni Likhacheva) A luxury automobile produced by the Likhachev auto factory and reserved for use only by the highest officials in the USSR.

zis The name of a Soviet car manufactured formerly by the Stalin auto factory; also used of contacts and associations that are useful to expediters. See **tolkach.**

Znanie The Soviet science or knowledge society.

zveno See **link.**

Appendix 1: Full and Candidate Members of the Politburo: 1917–87

THE TABLE that follows contains a list of past and current Politburo members (the latter as of mid-1987), together with selected biographical data. Current members are listed in **boldface** type.

Where we have found conflicting data (for example, different dates of entry into the Politburo), in most cases we have used the data supplied in the most recent source. For computation purposes those listed in office during one year alone are counted as having been in office a full year (even though they may have served but several months); those in office during two years as if for two full years, and so on.

In 1952 the name of the Politburo was changed to Presidium and the duties of the Orgburo and the Secretariat were combined. In 1966 the name Politburo was restored.

A question mark indicates the authors' estimate of nationality, family background, a date, and so on.

Where blank spaces appear we assume that the biographies we consulted would have included such data if it were pertinent.

The following notes should be borne in mind when using this appendix.

Family background. "Worker" is applied to those who were born in an urban area, or who are designated in the biographies as such; "intellectual" denotes offspring of clergy, engineers, gentry, teachers, or white-collar employees; "peasant" applies to those born in villages or designated in the biographies as such.

Nationality is determined by name or designation, or by republic of birth.

Tenure on Politburo indicates the years during which the member was an *active* member. Those who served on the Politburo only during a specific meeting of a party congress have not been included.

Other high positions concerns membership in one or more of these organs at some time during the member's career.

Yes indicates that during an individual's political career, along with being a candidate or full member of the Politburo or a member of the Secretariat, he or she also was a member of the party or state organ designated.

In the last column, *Yes* indicates membership in the Council of Ministers. For those in the Gorbachev administration, the first entry in the last column is the most important post or responsibility held as of 1987. In most cases the individual no longer holds the second or third post listed.

Name	*Family Background*	*Nationality*
Aliev, Geidar Alievich (1923–)	Worker	Azerbaijani
Andreev, Andrei Andreevich (1895–1971)	Peasant	Russian
Andrianov, Vasilii Mikhailovich (1902–?)	Worker?	Russian
Andropov, Yurii Vladimirovich (1914–84)	Worker?	Russian
Aristov, Averkii Borisovich (1903–73)	Worker?	Russian
Bagriov, Mir Dzhafar Abbasovich (1896–1956)	Worker?	Azerbaijani
Belyaev, Nikolai Il'ich (1903–66)	Peasant	Russian?
Beriya, Lavrentii Pavlovich (1893–1953)	Peasant	Georgian
Brezhnev, Leonid Il'ich (1906–82)	Worker?	Russian
Bubnov, Andrei Sergeevich (1883–1940)	Worker?	Russian
Bukharin, Nikolai Ivanovich (1888–1938)	Intellectual	Russian

Tenure on Politburo or Presidium		*Other High Positions*		
Candidate Member	*Full Member*	*Secretariat or Orgburo*	*Presidium of Supreme Soviet*	*Council of Ministers or Other*
76–82	82–	—	—	First deputy chairman, Council of Ministers; KGB; NKVD; MVD
27–34	34–52?	Yes	Yes	Agriculture Trade union leader
—	52–53	—	—	First secretary, Leningrad
67–73	73–84	First or general secretary, CPSU	President	Yes; KGB
—	52–53; 57–61	Yes	—	Komsomol; ambassador; trade union leader
53–53	—	—	Yes	MVD
—	57–60	Yes	Yes	—
39–46	46–53	—	—	MVD
52–53; 56–57	57–82	First or general secretary, CPSU	President	Yes
—	17–19?	Yes	—	—
19–20	20–29	—	—	Edited *Pravda*

Name	*Family Background*	*Nationality*
Bulganin, Nikolai Aleksandrovich (1895–1975)	Worker?	Russian
Chebrikov, Viktor Mikhailovich (1923–)	Worker?	Russian
Chernenko, Konstantin Ustinovich (1911–85)	Peasant	Russian
Chesnokov, Dmitrii Ivanovich (1910–73)	Worker?	Russian
Chubar, Vlas Yakovlevich (1891–1939)	Peasant	Ukrainian?
Demichev, Petr Nilovich (1918–)	Worker	Russian
Dolgikh, Vladimir Ivanovich (1924–)	Intellectual	Russian
Dzerzhinskiy, Feliks Edmundovich (1877–1926)	Intellectual	Polish?
Eltsin, Boris Nikolaevich (1931–)	Worker?	Russian
Efremov [Yefremov], Leonid Nikolaevich (1912–)	Worker?	Russian
Eykhe, Robert Indrikovich (1890–1940)	Peasant	Latvian

Tenure on Politburo or Presidium		*Other High Positions*		
Candidate Member	*Full Member*	*Secretariat or Orgburo*	*Presidium of Supreme Soviet*	*Council of Ministers or Other*
46–48	48–58	—	—	Prime minister; agitation and propaganda department
83–85	85–	—	—	Chairman, KGB
77–78	78–85	First or general secretary, CPSU	President	—
—	52–53	—	—	Edited *Kommunist*
27–35	35–37?	—	—	—
64–	—	—	Yes	Deputy chairman, Presidium Supreme Soviet; Minister of culture; first secretary, Moscow
82–	—	Yes	—	—
24–26	—	—	—	Cheka
86–	—	—	Yes	First secretary, Moscow
62–66	—	—	—	—
35–37?	—	—	Yes	—

Name	*Family Background*	*Nationality*
Frunze, Mikhail Vasil'yevich (1885–1925)	Worker	Ukrainian?
Furtseva, Ekaterina Alekseevna (1910–74)	Worker	Russian
Gorbachev, Mikhail Sergeevich (1931–)	Peasant	Russian
Grechko, Andrei Antonovich (1903–76)	Peasant	Ukrainian
Grishin, Viktor Vasil'evich (1914–)	Worker	Russian
Gromyko, Andrei Andreevich (1909–)	Peasant	Russian
Ignatov, Nikolai Grigor'evich (1901–66)	Peasant	Russian
Ignat'yev, Semen Denisovich (1904–)	Worker?	Tatar?
Kabanov, Ivan Grigor'evich (1898–1972)	Worker?	Russian?
Kaganovich, Lazar Moissevich (1893–?)	Peasant	Jewish
Kalinin, Mikhail Ivanovich (1875–1946)	Peasant	Russian
Kalnberzin, Yan Eduardovich (1893–?)	Worker?	Latvian

Tenure on Politburo or Presidium		*Other High Positions*		
Candidate Member	*Full Member*	*Secretariat or Orgburo*	*Presidium of Supreme Soviet*	*Council of Ministers or Other*
24–25	—	—	—	Chief of staff, Red Army
56–57	57–61	—	—	Minister of culture
79–80	80–	First or general secretary, CPSU	Yes	Chairman, USSR Council of Defense
—	73–76	—	—	Minister of defense
61–71	71–86	—	Yes	—
—	73–	—	President	Chairman, Presidium Supreme Soviet; Foreign minister; ambassador
52–53	57–61	Yes	—	Yes
—	52–53	Yes	Yes	MVD
53–58	—	—	—	—
27–30	30–57	Yes	—	Yes
19–26?	26–46?	—	—	President
57–61	—	—	—	Diplomat

Name	*Family Background*	*Nationality*
Kamenev, Lev Borisovich (1883–1936)	Intellectual	Jewish
Khrushchev, Nikita Sergeevich (1894–1971)	Peasant	Russian
Kirichenko, Aleksey Illarionovich (1908–75)	Peasant	Ukrainian
Kirilenko, Andrei Pavlovich (1906–)	Peasant	Russian
Kirov, Sergei Mironovich (1886–1934)	Worker?	Russian
Kiselev, Tikhon Yakovlevich (1917–)	Worker?	Belorussian
Korotchenko, Dem'yan Sergeevich (1894–1969)	Peasant	Ukrainian
Kosior, Stanislav Vikent'yevich (1889–1939)	Worker	Polish
Kosygin, Aleksey Nikolaevich (1904–80)	Worker?	Russian
Kozlov, Frol Romanovich (1908–65)	Peasant	Russian
Krestinskiy, Nikolai Nikolaevich (1888–1938)	Worker?	Russian
Kulakov, Fedor Davydovich (1918–78)	Worker?	Russian

Tenure on Politburo or Presidium		*Other High Positions*		
Candidate Member	*Full Member*	*Secretariat or Orgburo*	*Presidium of Supreme Soviet*	*Council of Ministers or Other*
26–27	17–26	—	President	—
35–39	39–64	First or general secretary, CPSU	—	Prime minister
53–55	55–60	Yes	—	—
57–61	62–82	Yes	—	—
27–34	34–34	Yes	Yes	—
80–84	—	Yes	—	—
57–61	52–53	—	Yes	—
27–30	30–39?	Yes	Yes	—
46–48; 57–60	48–52; 60–80	—	—	Prime minister; Gosplan
57–57	57–64	Yes	Yes	Yes
—	19–20	Yes	—	—
—	71–78	Yes	—	Yes

Name	Family Background	Nationality
Kunaev, Dinmukhamed Akhmedovich (1912–)	Intellectual	Kazakh
Kuusinen, Otto Vil'gel'movich (1881–1964)	Worker?	Finnish
Kuybyshev, Valerian Vladimirovich (1888–1935)	Intellectual	Russian
Kuznetsov, Vasilii Vasil'evich (1901–)	Peasant	Russian
Lenin, Vladimir Il'ich (1870–1924)	Intellectual	Russian
Ligachev, Egor Kuz'mich (1920–)	Worker	Russian
Malenkov, Georgii Maksimilianovich (1902–)	Worker?	Russian
Malyshev, Vyacheslav Aleksandrovich (1902–57)	Intellectual	Russian
Masherov, Petr Mironovich (1918–80)	Peasant	Belorussian
Mazurov, Kirill Trofimovich (1914–)	Peasant	Belorussian
Mel'nikov, Leonid Georgievich (1906–81)	Worker?	Russian
Mikhailov, Nikolai Aleksandrovich (1906–82)	Worker?	Russian

Tenure on Politburo or Presidium		*Other High Positions*		
Candidate Member	*Full Member*	*Secretariat or Orgburo*	*Presidium of Supreme Soviet*	*Council of Ministers or Other*
66–71	71–87	—	Yes	First secretary, Kazakhstan
—	52–53; 57–64	Yes	Yes	President, Karelo-Finnish SSR
—	27–35	Yes	—	Yes; Gosplan
44–52; 77–85	52–53	Yes	Yes	Ambassador; trade union leader
—	17–24	First or general secretary, CPSU	—	Prime minister
—	85–	Yes	—	Chairman, Foreign Affairs Commission, Soviet of the Union
41–46	46–57	First or general secretary, CPSU	—	Prime minister; agitation and propaganda department
—	52–53	—	—	Yes
66–80	—	—	Yes	Komsomol
57–65	65–78	—	—	—
53–56	52–53	—	—	Yes
—	52–53	Yes	—	Agitation and propaganda department; Komsomol; ambassador

Name	*Family Background*	*Nationality*
Mikoyan, Anastas Ivanovich (1895–1978)	Peasant	Armenian
Molotov, Vyacheslav Mikhailovich (1890–1986)	Peasant	Russian
Mukhitdinov, Nuritdin Akramovich (1917–)	Worker	Uzbek?
Mzhavandadze, Vasilii Pavlovich (1902–)	Worker?	Georgian
Nikonov, Viktor Petrovich (1929–)	Peasant	Russian
Ordzhonikidze, Grigorii Konstantinovich (1886–1937)	Peasant	Georgian?
Patolichev, Nikolai Semenovich (1908–)	Peasant	Russian
Pegov, Nikolai Mikhailovich (1905–)	Worker	Russian
Pel'she, Arvid Yanovich (1899–1983)	Worker?	Latvian
Pervukhin, Mikhail Georgievich (1904–78)	Worker?	Russian
Petrovskiy, Grigorii Ivanovich (1878–1958)	Worker	Ukrainian
Podgorny, Nikolai Viktorovich (1903–83)	Worker?	Ukrainian

Tenure on Politburo or Presidium		*Other High Positions*		
Candidate Member	*Full Member*	*Secretariat or Orgburo*	*Presidium of Supreme Soviet*	*Council of Ministers or Other*
26–35	35–66	—	President	Yes
24?–26	26–57	Yes	Yes	Prime minister; foreign minister
56–57	57–61	Yes	—	Diplomat
57–72	—	—	—	Diplomat
—	87–	Yes	—	Deputy chairman, Commission on the Agro-industrial Complex, Soviet of Nationalities
26–30	30–37	Yes	—	Yes
52–53	—	—	Yes	Diplomat
53–56	—	—	—	Ambassador
—	66–82	—	—	Diplomat
57–61	52–57	—	—	Yes; ambassador; Komsomol
26–39	—	—	Yes	—
58–60	60–77	Yes	President	—

Name	*Family Background*	*Nationality*
Polyansky, Dmitrii Stepanivich (1917–)	Peasant	Ukrainian
Ponamarev, Boris Nikolaevich (1905–)	Intellectual	Russian
Ponomarenko, Panteleimon Kondrat'evich (1902–84)	Worker?	Russian
Pospelov, Petr Nikolaevich (1898–1979)	Worker?	Russian
Postyshev, Pavel Petrovich (1887–1940)	Worker	Ukrainian
Preobrazhenskiy, Yevgeniy Alekseyevich (1886–1937)	Intellectual	Russian
Puzanov, Aleksandr Mikhailovich (1906–)	Peasant	Russian
Rashidov, Sharaf Rashidovich (1917–83)	Worker?	Uzbek
Romanov, Grigorii Vasil'evich (1923–)	Peasant	Russian
Rudzutak, Yan Ernestovich (1887–1938)	Peasant	Latvian?
Rykov, Aleksey Ivanovich (1881–1938)	Worker?	Russian
Ryzhkov, Nikolai Ivanovich (1929–)	Worker	Russian?
Saburov, Maksim Zakharovich (1900–)	Worker?	Russian

Tenure on Politburo or Presidium		*Other High Positions*		
Candidate Member	*Full Member*	*Secretariat or Orgburo*	*Presidium of Supreme Soviet*	*Council of Ministers or Other*
58–60	60–76	—	—	Yes; ambassador
72–86	—	Yes	—	—
53–56	52–53	Yes	—	Ambassador
57–61	—	Yes	—	Edited *Pravda*
34–35	—	—	Yes	—
—	20–21?	—	—	Edited *Pravda*
57–62	—	Yes	—	Ambassador
61–84	—	—	—	Diplomat
73–76	76–85	Yes	Yes	First secretary, Leningrad
24?–26; 34–37	26–32	—	Yes	Yes
—	24–30	Yes	—	Prime minister
—	85–	Yes	—	Prime minister
—	52–57	—	—	Gosplan; Komsomol

Name	*Family Background*	*Nationality*
Serebryakov, Leonid Petrovich (1890–1937)	Worker	Russian
Shcherbakov, Aleksandr Sergeevich (1901–45)	Worker	Russian
Shcherbitsky, Vladimir Vasil'evich (1918–)	Worker	Ukrainian
Shelepin, Aleksandr Nikolaevich (1918–)	Worker?	Russian
Shelest, Petr Efimovich (1908–)	Worker?	Ukrainian
Shepilov, Dmitrii Trofimovich (1905–)	Worker?	Russian?
Shevardnadze, Eduard Amvrosievich (1928–)	Worker?	Georgian
Shkiryatov, Matevi Mikhailovich (1883–1954)	Worker?	Russian
Shvernik, Nikolai Mikhailovich (1888–1970)	Worker?	Russian
Slyunkov, Nikolai Nikitaovich (1929–)	Peasant	Belorussian
Sokol'nikov, Grigorii Yakovlevich (1888–1939)	Worker?	Russian
Sokolov, Sergei Leonidovich (1911–)	Intellectual	Russian

Tenure on Politburo or Presidium		*Other High Positions*		
Candidate Member	*Full Member*	*Secretariat or Orgburo*	*Presidium of Supreme Soviet*	*Council of Ministers or Other*
—	20–21?	Yes	—	Yes
41–45	—	—	—	Yes; Komsomol
61–63; 65–71	71–	—	Yes	First secretary, Ukraine
—	64–75	Yes	—	KGB; Komsomol
63–64	64–73	—	—	Diplomat
56–57	—	Yes	—	Yes; edited *Pravda*; foreign minister
78–85	85–	—	—	Foreign minister; MVD; Komsomol; first secretary, Georgia
—	52–53	—	—	—
39–52; 53–57	52–53; 57–64	—	President	Trade union leader
86–87	87–	Yes	Yes	First secretary, Belorussia
24–25	17–19?	—	—	Gosplan
85–87	—	—	—	Minister of defense

Name	*Family Background*	*Nationality*
Solomentsev, Mikhail Sergeevich (1913–)	Peasant	Russian
Solovev Yurii Filippovich (1925–)	Worker?	Russian
Stalin, Josif Vissarionovich (1879–1953)	Worker	Georgian
Suslov, Mikhail Andreevich (1902–82)	Peasant	Russian
Talyzin, Nikolai Vladimirovich (1929–)	Worker	Russian
Tevosyan, Ivan Fedorovich (1902–58)	Worker	Azerbaijani
Tikhonov, Nikolai Aleksandrovich (1905–)	Intellectual	Ukrainian
Tomsky, Mikhail Pavlovich (1880–1936)	Worker	Russian?
Trotsky, Lev Davidovich (1879–1940)	Intellectual	Jewish
Uglanov, Nikolai Aleksandrovich (1886–1940)	Peasant	Russian
Ustinov, Dmitrii Fedorovich (1908–84)	Worker	Russian
Voronov, Gennadii Ivanovich (1910–)	Peasant	Russian

Tenure on Politburo or Presidium		*Other High Positions*		
Candidate Member	*Full Member*	*Secretariat or Orgburo*	*Presidium of Supreme Soviet*	*Council of Ministers or Other*
71–83	83–	Yes	—	Chairman, Communist Party Control Committee
86–	—	—	—	First secretary, Leningrad
—	17–53	First or general secretary, CPSU	Yes	Prime minister
—	52–53; 55–82	Yes	Yes	Agitation and propaganda department
85–	—	—	—	Chairman, Gosplan; first deputy chairman, Council of Ministers
52–53	—	—	—	Yes; ambassador
78–79	79–86	—	—	Prime minister; Gosplan
—	22–29	—	—	Yes; trade union leader
—	17–26	Yes	—	Commissar for military affairs; foreign commissar
27–29	—	Yes	—	Yes
65–76	76–84	Yes	—	Minister of defense
61–61	61–73	Yes	—	—

Name	*Family Background*	*Nationality*
Voroshilov, Kliment Yefremovich (1881–1969)	Peasant	Russian
Vorotnikov, Vitalii Ivanovich (1926–)	Worker?	Russian
Voznesenskiy, Nikolai Alekseyevich (1903–50)	Intellectual	Russian
Vyshinsky, Andrei Yanuar'evich (1893–1954)	Worker?	Russian
Yakovlev, Aleksandr Nikolaevich (1923–)	Worker?	Russian
Yazov, Dmitrii T. (1923–)	Peasant	Russian
Yezhov, Nikolai Ivanovich (1895–1939)	Worker?	Russian?
Yudin, Pavel Fedorovich (1899–1968)	Peasant	Russian
Zaikov, Lev Nikolaevich (1923–)	Worker?	Russian
Zhdanov, Andrei Aleksandrovich (1896–1948)	Intellectual	Russian
Zhukov, Georgii Konstantinovich (1896–1974)	Peasant	Russian

Tenure on Politburo or Presidium		*Other High Positions*		
Candidate Member	*Full Member*	*Secretariat or Orgburo*	*Presidium of Supreme Soviet*	*Council of Ministers or Other*
—	26–60	Yes	President	Yes
83–83	83–	—	—	Prime minister, RSFSR; ambassador
41–47	47–49	—	—	Yes; Gosplan
52–53	—	—	—	Foreign minister
87–87	87–	Yes	—	Agitation and propaganda department, Central Committee; Commission on Foreign Affairs, Council of Nationalities; first secretary, Leningrad; ambassador
87–	—	—	—	Minister of defense
37–38?	—	Yes	—	MVD
53–59	—	—	—	Ambassador
—	86–	Yes	Yes	Defense industry
35–39	39–48	Yes	—	Yes
56–57	57–57	—	—	Minister of defense

Name	*Family Background*	*Nationality*
Zinov'yev, Grigorii Yevseyevich (1883–1936)	Worker?	Russian
Zverev, Arsenii Grigor'evich (1900–69)	Peasant	Russian
Current Members of the Secretariat Not Politburo Members		
Biryukova, Aleksandra Pavlovna (1929–)	Peasant	Russian
Dobrynin, Anatolii Fedorovich (1919–)	Worker	Russian
Lukyanov, Anatolii Ivanovich (1930–)	Worker?	Russian
Medvedev, Vadim Andreevich (1929–)	Worker?	Russian
Razumovsky, Georgii Petrovich (1936–)	Worker?	Russian

Tenure on Politburo or Presidium		*Other High Positions*		
Candidate Member	*Full Member*	*Secretariat or Orgburo*	*Presidium of Supreme Soviet*	*Council of Ministers or Other*
—	17–20; 24–26	—	Yes	—
52–53	—	—	Yes	MVD
—	—	Yes	—	Secretary for consumer goods production, food industry and light industry, Central Committee; deputy chairman, Central Council of Trade Unions
—	—	Yes	—	Chief, International Department, Central Committee; chairman, Commission on Foreign Affairs, Soviet of Nationalities
—	—	Yes	—	Chief, General Department Central Committee
—	—	Yes	—	Chief, Department for Liaison with Communist and Workers' Parties of Socialist Countries, Central Committee
—	—	Yes	—	Chief, Department for Party Organizational Work, Central Committee;

Appendix 2: Constitution (Fundamental Law) of the Union of Soviet Socialist Republics

THE GREAT OCTOBER SOCIALIST REVOLUTION, made by the workers and peasants of Russia under the leadership of the Communist Party headed by Lenin, overthrew capitalist and landowner rule, broke the fetters of oppression, established the dictatorship of the proletariat, and created the Soviet state, a new type of state, the basic instrument for defending the gains of the revolution and for building socialism and communism. Humanity thereby began the epoch-making turn from capitalism to socialism.

After achieving victory in the Civil War and repulsing imperialist intervention, the Soviet government carried through far-reaching social and economic transformations, and put an end once and for all to exploitation of man by man, antagonisms between classes, and strife between nationalities. The unification of the Soviet Republics in the Union of Soviet Socialist Republics multiplied the forces and opportunities of the peoples of the country in the building of socialism. Social ownership of the means of production and genuine democracy for the working masses were established. For the first time in the history of mankind a socialist society was created.

The strength of socialism was vividly demonstrated by the immortal feat of the Soviet people and their Armed Forces in achieving their historic victory in the Great Patriotic War. This victory

Novosti Press Agency Publishing House Moscow, 1977

consolidated the influence and international standing of the Soviet Union and created new opportunities for growth of the forces of socialism, national liberation, democracy, and peace throughout the world.

Continuing their creative endeavours, the working people of the Soviet Union have ensured rapid, all-round development of the country and steady improvement of the socialist system. They have consolidated the alliance of the working class, collective-farm peasantry, and people's intelligentsia, and friendship of the nations and nationalities of the USSR. Socio-political and ideological unity of Soviet society, in which the working class is the leading force, has been achieved. The aims of the dictatorship of the proletariat having been fulfilled, the Soviet state has become a state of the whole people. The leading role of the Communist Party, the vanguard of all the people, has grown.

In the USSR a developed socialist society has been built. At this stage, when socialism is developing on its own foundations, the creative forces of the new system and the advantages of the socialist way of life are becoming increasingly evident, and the working people are more and more widely enjoying the fruits of their great revolutionary gains.

It is a society in which powerful productive forces and progressive science and culture have been created, in which the well-being of the people is constantly rising, and more and more favourable conditions are being provided for the all-round development of the individual.

It is a society of mature socialist social relations, in which, on the basis of the drawing together of all classes and social strata and of the juridical and factual equality of all its nations and nationalities and their fraternal co-operation, a new historical community of people has been formed—the Soviet people.

It is a society of high organisational capacity, ideological commitment, and consciousness of the working people, who are patriots and internationalists.

It is a society in which the law of life is concern of all for the good of each and concern of each for the good of all.

It is a society of true democracy, the political system of which ensures effective management of all public affairs, ever more active participation of the working people in running the state, and the combining of citizens' real rights and freedoms with their obligations and responsibility to society.

Developed socialist society is a natural, logical stage on the road to communism.

The supreme goal of the Soviet state is the building of a classless communist society in which there will be public, communist self-government. The main aims of the people's socialist state are: to lay the material and technical foundation of communism, to perfect socialist social relations and transform them into communist relations, to mould the citizen of communist society, to raise the people's living and cultural standards, to safeguard the country's security, and to further the consolidation of peace and development of international co-operation.

The Soviet people,

guided by the ideas of scientific communism and true to their revolutionary traditions,

relying on the great social, economic, and political gains of socialism,

striving for the further development of socialist democracy,

taking into account the international position of the USSR as part of the world system of socialism, and conscious of their internationalist responsibility,

preserving continuity of the ideas and principles of the first Soviet Constitution of 1918, the 1924 Constitution of the USSR and the 1936 Constitution of the USSR,

hereby affirm the principles of the social structure and policy of the USSR, and define the rights, freedoms and obligations of citizens, and the principles of the organisation of the socialist state of the whole people, and its aims, and proclaim these in this Constitution.

I. Principles of the Social Structure and Policy of the USSR

Chapter 1: The Political System

Article 1. The Union of Soviet Socialist Republics is a socialist state of the whole people, expressing the will and interests of the workers, peasants, and intelligentsia, the working people of all the nations and nationalities of the country.

Article 2. All power in the USSR belongs to the people.

The people exercise state power through Soviets of People's Deputies, which constitute the political foundation of the USSR.

All other state bodies are under the control of, and accountable to, the Soviets of People's Deputies.

Article 3. The Soviet state is organised and functions on the principle of democratic centralism, namely the electiveness of all bodies of state authority from the lowest to the highest, their accountability to the people, and the obligation of lower bodies to observe the decisions of higher ones. Democratic centralism combines central leadership with local initiative and creative activity and with the responsibility of each state body and official for the work entrusted to them.

Article 4. The Soviet state and all its bodies function on the basis of socialist law, ensure the maintenance of law and order, and safeguard the interests of society and the rights and freedoms of citizens.

State organisations, public organisations and officials shall observe the Constitution of the USSR and Soviet laws.

Article 5. Major matters of state shall be submitted to nationwide discussion and put to a popular vote (referendum).

Article 6. The leading and guiding force of Soviet society and the nucleus of its political system, of all state organisations and public organisations, is the Communist Party of the Soviet Union. The CPSU exists for the people and serves the people.

The Communist Party, armed with Marxism-Leninism, determines the general perspectives of the development of society and the course of the home and foreign policy of the USSR, directs the great constructive work of the Soviet people, and imparts a planned, systematic and theoretically substantiated character to their struggle for the victory of communism.

All party organisations shall function within the framework of the Constitution of the USSR.

Article 7. Trade unions, the All-Union Leninist Young Communist League, co-operatives, and other public organisations, participate, in accordance with the aims laid down in their rules, in managing state and public affairs, and in deciding political, economic, and social and cultural matters.

Article 8. Work collectives take part in discussing and deciding state and public affairs, in planning production and social development, in training and placing personnel, and in discussing and deciding matters pertaining to the management of enterprises and institutions, the improvement of working and living conditions, and the use of funds allocated both for developing production and for social and cultural purposes and financial incentives.

Work collectives promote socialist emulation, the spread of progressive methods of work, and the strengthening of production discipline, educate their members in the spirit of communist morality, and strive to enhance their political consciousness and raise their cultural level and skills and qualifications.

Article 9. The principal direction in the development of the political system of Soviet society is the extension of socialist democracy, namely ever broader participation of citizens in managing the affairs of society and the state, continuous improvement of the machinery of state, heightening of the activity of public organisations, strengthening of the system of people's control, consolidation of the legal foundations of the functioning of the state and of public life, greater openness and publicity, and constant responsiveness to public opinion.

Chapter 2: The Economic System

Article 10. The foundation of the economic system of the USSR is socialist ownership of the means of production in the form of state property (belonging to all the people), and collective farm-and-co-operative property.

Socialist ownership also embraces the property of trade unions and other public organisations which they require to carry out their purposes under their rules.

The state protects socialist property and provides conditions for its growth.

No one has the right to use socialist property for personal gain or other selfish ends.

Article 11. State property, i.e., the common property of the Soviet people, is the principal form of socialist property.

The land, its minerals, waters, and forests are the exclusive property of the state. The state owns the basic means of production in industry, construction, and agriculture; means of transport and communication; the banks; the property of state-run trade organisations and public utilities, and other state-run undertakings; most urban housing; and other property necessary for state purposes.

Article 12. The property of collective farms and other co-operative organisations, and of their joint undertakings, comprises the means of production and other assets which they require for the purposes laid down in their rules.

The land held by collective farms is secured to them for their free use in perpetuity.

The state promotes development of collective farm-and-co-operative property and its approximation to state property.

Collective farms, like other land users, are obliged to make effective and thrifty use of the land and to increase its fertility.

Article 13. Earned income forms the basis of the personal property of Soviet citizens. The personal property of citizens of the USSR may include articles of everyday use, personal consumption and convenience, the implements and other objects of a small-holding, a house, and earned savings. The personal property of citizens and the right to inherit it are protected by the state.

Citizens may be granted the use of plots of land, in the manner prescribed by law, for a subsidiary small-holding (including the keeping of livestock and poultry), for fruit and vegetable growing or for building an individual dwelling. Citizens are required to make rational use of the land allotted to them. The state, and collective farms provide assistance to citizens in working their small-holdings.

Property owned or used by citizens shall not serve as a means of deriving unearned income or be employed to the detriment of the interests of society.

Article 14. The source of the growth of social wealth and of the well-being of the people, and of each individual, is the labour, free from exploitation, of Soviet people.

The state exercises control over the measure of labour and of consumption in accordance with the principle of socialism: "From each according to his ability, to each according to his work." It fixes the rate of taxation on taxable income.

Socially useful work and its results determine a person's status in society. By combining material and moral incentives and encouraging innovation and a creative attitude to work, the state helps transform labour into the prime vital need of every Soviet citizen.

Article 15. The supreme goal of social production under socialism is the fullest possible satisfaction of the people's growing material, and cultural and intellectual requirements.

Relying on the creative initiative of the working people, socialist emulation, and scientific and technological progress, and by improving the forms and methods of economic management, the state ensures growth of the productivity of labour, raising of the efficiency of production and of the quality of work, and dynamic, planned, proportionate development of the economy.

Article 16. The economy of the USSR is an integral economic complex comprising all the elements of social production, distribution, and exchange on its territory.

The economy is managed on the basis of state plans for economic and social development, with due account of the sectoral and territorial principles, and by combining centralised direction with the managerial independence and initiative of individual and amalgamated enterprises and other organisations, for which active use is made of management accounting, profit, cost, and other economic levers and incentives.

Article 17. In the USSR, the law permits individual labour in handicrafts, farming, the provision of services for the public, and other forms of activity based exclusively on the personal work of individual citizens and members of their families. The state makes regulations for such work to ensure that it serves the interests of society.

Article 18. In the interests of the present and future generations, the necessary steps are taken in the USSR to protect and make scientific, rational use of the land and its mineral and water resources, and the plant and animal kingdoms, to preserve the purity of air and water, ensure reproduction of natural wealth, and improve the human environment.

Chapter 3: Social Development and Culture

Article 19. The social basis of the USSR is the unbreakable alliance of the workers, peasants, and intelligentsia.

The state helps enhance the social homogeneity of society, namely the elimination of class differences and of the essential distinctions between town and country and between mental and physical labour, and the all-round development and drawing together of all the nations and nationalities of the USSR.

Article 20. In accordance with the communist ideal—"The free development of each is the condition of the free development of all"—the state pursues the aim of giving citizens more and more real opportunities to apply their creative energies, abilities, and talents, and to develop their personalities in every way.

Article 21. The state concerns itself with improving working conditions, safety and labour protection and the scientific organisation of work, and with reducing and ultimately eliminating all arduous physical labour through comprehensive mechanisation and automation of production processes in all branches of the economy.

Article 22. A programme is being consistently implemented in the USSR to convert agricultural work into a variety of industrial work, to extend the network of educational, cultural and medical institutions, and of trade, public catering, service and public utility facilities in rural localities, and transform hamlets and villages into well-planned and well-appointed settlements.

Article 23. The state pursues a steady policy of raising people's pay levels and real incomes through increase in productivity.

In order to satisfy the needs of Soviet people more fully social consumption funds are created. The state, with the broad participation of public organisations and work collectives, ensures the growth and just distribution of these funds.

Article 24. In the USSR, state systems of health protection, social security, trade and public catering, communal services and amenities, and public utilities, operate and are being extended.

The state encourages co-operatives and other public organisations to provide all types of services for the population. It encourages the development of mass physical culture and sport.

Article 25. In the USSR there is a uniform system of public education, which is being constantly improved, that provides general education and vocational training for citizens, serves the communist education and intellectual and physical development of the youth, and trains them for work and social activity.

Article 26. In accordance with society's needs the state provides for planned development of science and the training of scientific personnel and organises introduction of the results of research in the economy and other spheres of life.

Article 27. The state concerns itself with protecting, augmenting and making extensive use of society's cultural wealth for the moral and aesthetic education of the Soviet people, for raising their cultural level.

In the USSR development of the professional, amateur and folk arts is encouraged in every way.

Chapter 4: Foreign Policy

Article 28. The USSR steadfastly pursues a Leninist policy of peace and stands for strengthening of the security of nations and broad international co-operation.

The foreign policy of the USSR is aimed at ensuring international conditions favourable for building communism in the USSR, safeguarding the state interests of the Soviet Union, consolidating the positions of world socialism, supporting the struggle of peoples for national liberation and social progress, preventing wars of aggression, achieving universal and complete disarmament, and consistently implementing the principle of the peaceful coexistence of states with different social systems.

In the USSR war propaganda is banned.

Article 29. The USSR's relations with other states are based on observance of the following principles: sovereign equality; mutual renunciation of the use or threat of force; inviolability of frontiers; territorial integrity of states; peaceful settlement of disputes; non-intervention in internal affairs; respect for human rights and fundamental freedoms; the equal rights of peoples and their right to decide their own destiny; co-operation among states; and fulfilment in good faith of obligations arising from the generally recognised principles and rules of international law, and from the international treaties signed by the USSR.

Article 30. The USSR, as part of the world system of socialism and of the socialist community, promotes and strengthens friendship, co-operation, and comradely mutual assistance with other socialist countries on the basis of the principle of socialist internationalism, and takes an active part in socialist economic integration and the socialist international division of labour.

Chapter 5: Defence of the Socialist Motherland

Article 31. Defence of the Socialist Motherland is one of the most important functions of the state, and is the concern of the whole people.

In order to defend the gains of socialism, the peaceful labour of the Soviet people, and the sovereignty and territorial integrity of the state, the USSR maintains armed forces and has instituted universal military service.

The duty of the Armed Forces of the USSR to the people is to provide reliable defence of the Socialist Motherland and to be in constant combat readiness, guaranteeing that any aggressor is instantly repulsed.

Article 32. The state ensures the security and defence capability of the country, and supplies the Armed Forces of the USSR with everything necessary for that purpose.

The duties of state bodies, public organisations, officials, and citizens in regard to safeguarding the country's security and strengthening its defence capacity are defined by the legislation of the USSR.

II. The State and the Individual

Chapter 6: Citizenship of the USSR. Equality of Citizens' Rights

Article 33. Uniform federal citizenship is established for the USSR. Every citizen of a Union Republic is a citizen of the USSR.

The grounds and procedure for acquiring or forfeiting Soviet citizenship are defined by the Law on Citizenship of the USSR.

When abroad, citizens of the USSR enjoy the protection and assistance of the Soviet state.

Article 34. Citizens of the USSR are equal before the law, without distinction of origin, social or property status, race or nationality, sex, education, language, attitude to religion, type and nature of occupation, domicile, or other status.

The equal rights of citizens of the USSR are guaranteed in all fields of economic, political, social, and cultural life.

Article 35. Women and men have equal rights in the USSR.

Exercise of these rights is ensured by according women equal access with men to education and vocational and professional training, equal opportunities in employment, remuneration, and promotion, and in social and political, and cultural activity, and by special labour and health protection measures for women; by providing conditions enabling mothers to work; by legal protection, and material and moral support for mothers and children, including paid leaves and other benefits for expectant mothers and mothers, and gradual reduction of working time for mothers with small children.

Article 36. Citizens of the USSR of different races and nationalities have equal rights.

Exercise of these rights is ensured by a policy of all-round development and drawing together of all the nations and nationalities of the USSR, by educating citizens in the spirit of Soviet patriotism and socialist internationalism, and by the possibility to use their native language and the languages of other peoples of the USSR.

Any direct or indirect limitation of the rights of citizens or establishment of direct or indirect privileges on grounds of race or nationality, and any advocacy of racial or national exclusiveness, hostility or contempt, are punishable by law.

Article 37. Citizens of other countries and stateless persons in the USSR are guaranteed the rights and freedoms provided by law, including the right to apply to a court and other state bodies for the protection of their personal, property, family, and other rights.

Citizens of other countries and stateless persons, when in the USSR, are obliged to respect the Constitution of the USSR and observe Soviet laws.

Article 38. The USSR grants the right of asylum to foreigners persecuted for defending the interests of the working people and the cause of peace, or for participation in the revolutionary and national-liberation movement, or for progressive social and political, scientific or other creative activity.

Chapter 7: The Basic Rights, Freedoms, and Duties of Citizens of the USSR

Article 39. Citizens of the USSR enjoy in full the social, economic, political and personal rights and freedoms proclaimed and guaranteed by the Constitution of the USSR and by Soviet laws. The socialist system ensures enlargement of the rights and freedoms of citizens and continuous improvement of their living standards as social, economic, and cultural development programmes are fulfilled.

Enjoyment by citizens of their rights and freedoms must not be to the detriment of the interests of society or the state, or infringe the rights of other citizens.

Article 40. Citizens of the USSR have the right to work (that is, to guaranteed employment and pay in accordance with the quantity and quality of their work, and not below the state-established minimum), including the right to choose their trade or profession, type of job and work in accordance with their inclinations, abilities, training and education, with due account of the needs of society.

This right is ensured by the socialist economic system, steady growth of the productive forces, free vocational and professional training, improvement of skills, training in new trades or professions, and development of the systems of vocational guidance and job placement.

Article 41. Citizens of the USSR have the right to rest and leisure.

This right is ensured by the establishment of a working week not exceeding 41 hours, for workers and other employees, a shorter working day in a number of trades and industries, and shorter hours for night work; by the provision of paid annual holidays, weekly days of rest, extension of the network of cultural, educational and health-building institutions, and the development on a mass scale of sport, physical culture, and camping and tourism; by the provision of neighbourhood recreational facilities, and of other opportunities for rational use of free time.

The length of collective farmers' working and leisure time is established by their collective farms.

Article 42. Citizens of the USSR have the right to health protection.

This right is ensured by free, qualified medical care provided by state health institutions; by extension of the network of therapeutic and health-building institutions; by the development and improvement of safety and hygiene in industry; by carrying out broad prophylactic measures; by measures to improve the environment; by special care for the health of the rising generation, including prohibition of child labour, excluding the work done by children as part of the school curriculum; and by developing research to prevent and reduce the incidence of disease and ensure citizens a long and active life.

Article 43. Citizens of the USSR have the right to maintenance in old age, in sickness, and in the event of complete or partial disability or loss of the breadwinner.

This right is guaranteed by social insurance of workers and other employees and collective farmers; by allowances for temporary disability; by the provision by the state or by collective farms of retirement pensions, disability pensions, and pensions for loss of the breadwinner; by providing employment for the partially disabled; by care for the elderly and the disabled; and by other forms of social security.

Article 44. Citizens of the USSR have the right to housing.

This right is ensured by the development and upkeep of state and socially-owned housing; by assistance for co-operative and individual house building; by fair distribution, under public control, of the housing that becomes available through fulfilment of the programme of building well-appointed dwellings, and by low rents and low charges for utility services. Citizens of the USSR shall take good care of the housing allocated to them.

Article 45. Citizens of the USSR have the right to education.

This right is ensured by free provision of all forms of education, by the institution of universal, compulsory secondary education, and broad development of vocational, specialised secondary, and higher education, in which instruction is oriented toward practical activity and production; by the development of extramural, correspondence and evening courses; by the provision of state scholarships and grants and privileges for students; by the free issue of school textbooks; by the opportunity to attend a school where teaching is in the native language; and by the provision of facilities for self-education.

Article 46. Citizens of the USSR have the right to enjoy cultural benefits.

This right is ensured by broad access to the cultural treasures of their own land and of the world that are preserved in state and other public collections; by the development and fair distribution of cultural and educational institutions throughout the country; by developing television and radio broadcasting and the publishing of books, newspapers and periodicals, and by extending the free library service; and by expanding cultural exchanges with other countries.

Article 47. Citizens of the USSR, in accordance with the aims of building communism, are guaranteed freedom of scientific, technical, and artistic work. This freedom is ensured by broadening scientific research, encouraging invention and innovation, and developing literature and the arts. The state provides the necessary material conditions for this and support for voluntary societies and unions of workers in the arts, organises introduction of inventions and innovations in production and other spheres of activity.

The rights of authors, inventors and innovators are protected by the state.

Article 48. Citizens of the USSR have the right to take part in the management and administration of state and public affairs and in the discussion and adoption of laws and measures of All-Union and local significance.

This right is ensured by the opportunity to vote and to be elected to Soviets of People's Deputies and other elective state bodies, to take part in nationwide discussions and referendums, in people's control, in the work of state bodies, public organisations, and local community groups, and in meetings at places of work or residence.

Article 49. Every citizen of the USSR has the right to submit proposals to state bodies and public organisations for improving their activity, and to criticise shortcomings in their work.

Officials are obliged, within established time-limits, to examine citizens' proposals and requests, to reply to them, and to take appropriate action.

Persecution for criticism is prohibited. Persons guilty of such persecution shall be called to account.

Article 50. In accordance with the interests of the people and in order to strengthen and develop the socialist system, citizens of the USSR are guaranteed freedom of speech, of the press, and of assembly, meetings, street processions and demonstrations.

Exercise of these political freedoms is ensured by putting public buildings, streets and squares at the disposal of the working people and their organisations, by broad dissemination of information, and by the opportunity to use the press, television, and radio.

Article 51. In accordance with the aims of building communism, citizens of the USSR have the right to associate in public organisations that promote their political activity and initiative and satisfaction of their various interests.

Public organisations are guaranteed conditions for successfully performing the functions defined in their rules.

Article 52. Citizens of the USSR are guaranteed freedom of conscience, that is, the right to profess or not to profess any religion, and to conduct religious worship or atheistic propaganda. Incitement of hostility or hatred on religious grounds is prohibited.

In the USSR, the church is separated from the state, and the school from the church.

Article 53. The family enjoys the protection of the state.

Marriage is based on the free consent of the woman and the man; the spouses are completely equal in their family relations.

The state helps the family by providing and developing a broad system of child-care institutions, by organising and improving communal services and public catering, by paying grants on the birth of a child, by providing children's allowances and benefits for large families, and other forms of family allowances and assistance.

Article 54. Citizens of the USSR are guaranteed inviolability of the person. No one may be arrested except by a court decision or on the warrant of a procurator.

Article 55. Citizens of the USSR are guaranteed inviolability of the home. No one may, without lawful grounds, enter a home against the will of those residing in it.

Article 56. The privacy of citizens, and of their correspondence, telephone conversations, and telegraphic communications is protected by law.

Article 57. Respect for the individual and protection of the rights and freedoms of citizens are the duty of all state bodies, public organisations, and officials.

Citizens of the USSR have the right to protection by the courts against encroachments on their honour and reputation, life and health, and personal freedom and property.

Article 58. Citizens of the USSR have the right to lodge a complaint against the actions of officials, state bodies and public bodies. Complaints shall be examined according to the procedure and within the time-limit established by law.

Actions by officials that contravene the law or exceed their powers, and infringe the rights of citizens, may be appealed against in a court in the manner prescribed by law.

Citizens of the USSR have the right to compensation for damage resulting from unlawful actions by state organisations and public organisations, or by officials in the performance of their duties.

Article 59. Citizens' exercise of their rights and freedoms is inseparable from the performance of their duties and obligations.

Citizens of the USSR are obliged to observe the Constitution of the USSR and Soviet laws, comply with the standards of socialist conduct, and uphold the honour and dignity of Soviet citizenship.

Article 60. It is the duty of, and a matter of honour for, every able-bodied citizen of the USSR to work conscientiously in his chosen, socially useful occupation, and strictly to observe labour discipline. Evasion of socially useful work is incompatible with the principles of socialist society.

Article 61. Citizens of the USSR are obliged to preserve and protect socialist property. It is the duty of a citizen of the USSR to combat misappropriation and squandering of state and socially-owned property and to make thrifty use of the people's wealth.

Persons encroaching in any way on socialist property shall be punished according to the law.

Article 62. Citizens of the USSR are obliged to safeguard the interests of the Soviet state, and to enhance its power and prestige.

Defence of the Socialist Motherland is the sacred duty of every citizen of the USSR.

Betrayal of the Motherland is the gravest of crimes against the people.

Article 63. Military service in the ranks of the Armed Forces of the USSR is an honourable duty of Soviet citizens.

Article 64. It is the duty of every citizen of the USSR to respect the national dignity of other citizens, and to strengthen friendship of the nations and nationalities of the multinational Soviet state.

Article 65. A citizen of the USSR is obliged to respect the rights and lawful interests of other persons, to be uncompromising toward anti-social behaviour, and to help maintain public order.

Article 66. Citizens of the USSR are obliged to concern themselves with the upbringing of children, to train them for socially useful work, and to raise them as worthy members of socialist society. Children are obliged to care for their parents and help them.

Article 67. Citizens of the USSR are obliged to protect nature and conserve its riches.

Article 68. Concern for the preservation of historical monuments and other cultural values is a duty and obligation of citizens of the USSR.

Article 69. It is the internationalist duty of citizens of the USSR to promote friendship and co-operation with peoples of other lands and help maintain and strengthen world peace.

III. The National–State Structure of the USSR

Chapter 8: The USSR— A Federal State

Article 70. The Union of Soviet Socialist Republics is an integral, federal, multinational state formed on the principle of socialist federalism as a result of the free self-determination of nations and the voluntary association of equal Soviet Socialist Republics.

The USSR embodies the state unity of the Soviet people and draws all its nations and nationalities together for the purpose of jointly building communism.

Article 71. The Union of Soviet Socialist Republics unites:

the Russian Soviet Federative Socialist Republic,
the Ukrainian Soviet Socialist Republic,
the Byelorussian Soviet Socialist Republic,
the Uzbek Soviet Socialist Republic,
the Kazakh Soviet Socialist Republic,
the Georgian Soviet Socialist Republic,
the Azerbaijan Soviet Socialist Republic,
the Lithuanian Soviet Socialist Republic,
the Moldavian Soviet Socialist Republic,
the Latvian Soviet Socialist Republic,
the Kirghiz Soviet Socialist Republic,
the Tajik Soviet Socialist Republic,
the Armenian Soviet Socialist Republic,
the Turkmen Soviet Socialist Republic,
the Estonian Soviet Socialist Republic.

Article 72. Each Union Republic shall retain the right freely to secede from the USSR.

Article 73. The jurisdiction of the Union of Soviet Socialist Republics, as represented by its highest bodies of state authority and administration, shall cover:

1. the admission of new republics to the USSR; endorsement of the formation of new autonomous republics and autonomous regions within Union Republics;

2. determination of the state boundaries of the USSR and approval of changes in the boundaries between Union Republics;

3. establishment of the general principles for the organisation and functioning of republican and local bodies of state authority and administration;

4. the ensurance of uniformity of legislative norms throughout the USSR and establishment of the fundamentals of the legislation of the Union of Soviet Socialist Republics and Union Republics;

5. pursuance of a uniform social and economic policy; direction of the country's economy determination of the main lines of scientific and technological progress and the general measures for rational exploitation and conservation of natural resources; the drafting and approval of state plans for the economic and social development of the USSR, and endorsement of reports on their fulfilment;

6. the drafting and approval of the consolidated Budget of the USSR, and endorsement of the report on its execution; management of a single monetary and credit system; determination of the taxes and revenues forming the Budget of the USSR; and the formulation of prices and wages policy;

7. direction of the sectors of the economy, and of enterprises and amalgamations under Union jurisdiction, and general direction of industries under Union-Republican jurisdiction;

8. issues of war and peace, defence of the sovereignty of the USSR and safeguarding of its frontiers and territory, and organisation of defence; direction of the Armed Forces of the USSR;

9. state security;

10. representation of the USSR in international relations; the USSR's relations with other states and with international organisations; establishment of the general procedure for, and coordination of, the relations of Union Republics with other states and with international organisations; foreign trade and other forms of external economic activity on the basis of state monopoly;

11. control over observance of the Constitution of the USSR, and ensurance of conformity of the Constitutions of Union Republics to the Constitution of the USSR;

12. and settlement of other matters of All-Union importance.

Article 74. The laws of the USSR shall have the same force in all Union Republics. In the event of a discrepancy between a Union Republic law and an All-Union law, the law of the USSR shall prevail.

Article 75. The territory of the Union of Soviet Socialist Republics is a single entity and comprises the territories of the Union Republics.

The sovereignty of the USSR extends throughout its territory.

Chapter 9: The Union Soviet Socialist Republic

Article 76. A Union Republic is a sovereign Soviet socialist state that has united with other Soviet Republics in the Union of Soviet Socialist Republics.

Outside the spheres listed in Article 73 of the Constitution of the USSR, a Union Republic exercises independent authority on its territory.

A Union Republic shall have its own Constitution conforming to the Constitution of the USSR with the specific features of the Republic being taken into account.

Article 77. Union Republics take part in decision-making in the Supreme Soviet of the USSR, the Presidium of the Supreme Soviet of the USSR, the Government of the USSR, and other bodies of the Union of Soviet Socialist Republics in matters that come within the jurisdiction of the Union of Soviet Socialist Republics.

A Union Republic shall ensure comprehensive economic and social development on its territory, facilitate exercise of the powers of the USSR on its territory, and implement the decisions of the highest bodies of state authority and administration of the USSR.

In matters that come within its jurisdiction, a Union Republic shall co-ordinate and control the activity of enterprises, institutions, and organisations subordinate to the Union.

Article 78. The territory of a Union Republic may not be altered without its consent. The boundaries between Union Republics may be altered by mutual agreement of the Republics concerned, subject to ratification by the Union of Soviet Socialist Republics.

Article 79. A Union Republic shall determine its division into territories, regions, areas, and districts, and decide other matters relating to its administrative and territorial structure.

Article 80. A Union Republic has the right to enter into relations with other states, conclude treaties with them, exchange diplomatic and consular representatives, and take part in the work of international organisations.

Article 81. The sovereign rights of Union Republics shall be safeguarded by the USSR.

Chapter 10: The Autonomous Soviet Socialist Republic

Article 82. An Autonomous Republic is a constituent part of a Union Republic.

In spheres not within the jurisdiction of the Union of Soviet Socialist Republics and the Union Republic, an Autonomous Republic shall deal independently with matters within its jurisdiction.

An Autonomous Republic shall have its own Constitution conforming to the Constitutions of the USSR and the Union Republic with the specific features of the Autonomous Republic being taken into account.

Article 83. An Autonomous Republic takes part in decision-making through the highest bodies of state authority and administration of the USSR and of the Union Republic respectively, in matters that come within the jurisdiction of the USSR and the Union Republic.

An Autonomous Republic shall ensure comprehensive economic and social development on its territory, facilitate exercise of the powers of the USSR and the Union Republic on its territory, and implement decisions of the highest bodies of state authority and administration of the USSR and the Union Republic.

In matters within its jurisdiction, an Autonomous Republic shall co-ordinate and control the activity of enterprises, institutions, and organisations subordinate to the Union or the Union Republic.

Article 84. The territory of an Autonomous Republic may not be altered without its consent.

Article 85. The Russian Soviet Federative Socialist Republic includes the Bashkir, Buryat, Daghestan, Kabardin-Balkar, Kalmyk, Karelian, Komi, Mari, Mordovian, North Ossetian, Tatar, Tuva, Udmurt, Chechen-Ingush, Chuvash, and Yakut Autonomous Soviet Socialist Republics.

The Uzbek Soviet Socialist Republic includes the Kara-Kalpak Autonomous Soviet Socialist Republic.

The Georgian Soviet Socialist Republic includes the Abkhasian and Adzhar Autonomous Soviet Socialist Republics.

The Azerbaijan Soviet Socialist Republic includes the Nakhichevan Autonomous Soviet Socialist Republic.

Chapter 11: The Autonomous Region and Autonomous Area

Article 86. An Autonomous Region is a constituent part of a Union Republic or Territory. The Law on an Autonomous Region, upon submission by the Soviet of People's Deputies of the Autonomous Region concerned, shall be adopted by the Supreme Soviet of the Union Republic.

Article 87. The Russian Soviet Federative Socialist Republic includes the Adygei, Gorno-Altai, Jewish, Karachai-Circassian, and Khakass Autonomous Regions.

The Georgian Soviet Socialist Republic includes the South Ossetian Autonomous Region.

The Azerbaijan Soviet Socialist Republic includes the Nagorno-Karabakh Autonomous Region.

The Tajik Soviet Socialist Republic includes the Gorno-Badakhshan Autonomous Region.

Article 88. An Autonomous Area is a constituent part of a Territory or Region. The Law on an Autonomous Area shall be adopted by the Supreme Soviet of the Union Republic concerned.

IV Soviets of People's Deputies and Electoral Procedure

Chapter 12: The System of Soviets of People's Deputies and the Principles of Their Work

Article 89. The Soviets of People's Deputies, i.e. the Supreme Soviet of the USSR, the Supreme Soviets of Union Republics, the

Supreme Soviets of Autonomous Republics, the Soviets of People's Deputies of Territories and Regions, the Soviets of People's Deputies of Autonomous Regions and Autonomous Areas, and the Soviets of People's Deputies of districts, cities, city districts, settlements and villages shall constitute a single system of bodies of state authority.

Article 90. The term of the Supreme Soviet of the USSR, the Supreme Soviets of Union Republics, and the Supreme Soviets of Autonomous Republics shall be five years.

The term of local Soviets of People's Deputies shall be two and a half years.

Elections to Soviets of People's Deputies shall be called not later than two months before the expiry of the term of the Soviet concerned.

Article 91. The most important matters within the jurisdiction of the respective Soviets of People's Deputies shall be considered and settled at their sessions.

Soviets of People's Deputies shall elect standing commissions and form executive-administrative, and other bodies accountable to them.

Article 92. Soviets of People's Deputies shall form people's control bodies combining state control with control by the working people at enterprises, collective farms, institutions, and organisations.

People's control bodies shall check on the fulfilment of state plans and assignments, combat breaches of state discipline, localistic tendencies, narrow departmental attitudes, mismanagement, extravagance and waste, red tape and bureaucracy, and help improve the working of the state machinery.

Article 93. Soviets of People's Deputies shall direct all sectors of state, economic, and social and cultural development, either directly or through bodies instituted by them, take decisions and ensure their execution, and verify their implementation.

Article 94. Soviets of People's Deputies shall function publicly on the basis of collective, free, constructive discussion and decision-making, of systematic reporting back to them and the people by their executive-administrative and other bodies, and of involving citizens on a broad scale in their work.

Soviets of People's Deputies and the bodies set up by them shall systematically inform the public about their work and the decisions taken by them.

Chapter 13: The Electoral System

Article 95. Deputies to all Soviets shall be elected on the basis of universal, equal, and direct suffrage by secret ballot.

Article 96. Elections shall be universal: all citizens of the USSR who have reached the age of 18 shall have the right to vote and to be elected, with the exception of persons who have been legally certified insane.

To be eligible for election to the Supreme Soviet of the USSR a citizen of the USSR must have reached the age of 21.

Article 97. Elections shall be equal: each citizen shall have one vote; all voters shall exercise the franchise on an equal footing.

Article 98. Elections shall be direct: deputies to all Soviets of People's Deputies shall be elected by citizens by direct vote.

Article 99. Voting at elections shall be secret: control over voters' exercise of the franchise is inadmissible.

Article 100. The following shall have the right to nominate candidates: branches and organisations of the Communist Party of the Soviet Union, trade unions, and the All-Union Leninist Young Communist League; co-operatives and other public organisations; work collectives, and meetings of servicemen in their military units.

Citizens of the USSR and public organisations are guaranteed the right to free and all-round discussion of the political and personal qualities and competence of candidates, and the right to campaign for them at meetings, in the press, and on television and radio.

The expenses involved in holding elections to Soviets of People's Deputies shall be met by the state.

Article 101. Deputies to Soviets of People's Deputies shall be elected by constituencies.

A citizen of the USSR may not, as a rule, be elected to more than two Soviets of People's Deputies.

Elections to the Soviets shall be conducted by electoral commissions consisting of representatives of public organisations and work collectives, and of meetings of servicemen in military units.

The procedure for holding elections to Soviets of People's Deputies shall be defined by the laws of the USSR, and of Union and Autonomous Republics.

Article 102. Electors give mandates to their Deputies.

The appropriate Soviets of People's Deputies shall examine electors' mandates, take them into account in drafting economic and social development plans and in drawing up the budget, organise implementation of the mandates, and inform citizens about it.

Chapter 14: People's Deputies

Article 103. Deputies are the plenipotentiary representatives of the people in the Soviets of People's Deputies.

In the Soviets, Deputies deal with matters relating to state, economic, and social and cultural development, organise implementation of the decisions of the Soviets, and exercise control over the work of state bodies, enterprises, institutions and organisations.

Deputies shall be guided in their activities by the interests of the state, and shall take the needs of their constituents into account and work to implement their electors' mandates.

Article 104. Deputies shall exercise their powers without discontinuing their regular employment or duties.

During sessions of the Soviet, and so as to exercise their deputy's powers in other cases stipulated by law, Deputies shall be released from their regular employment or duties, with retention of their average earnings at their permanent place of work.

Article 105. A Deputy has the right to address inquiries to the appropriate state bodies and officials, who are obliged to reply to them at a session of the Soviet.

Deputies have the right to approach any state or public body, enterprise, institution, or organisation on matters arising from their work as Deputies and to take part in considering the questions raised by them. The heads of the state or public bodies, enterprises, institutions or organisations concerned are obliged to receive Deputies without delay and to consider their proposals within the time-limit established by law.

Article 106. Deputies shall be ensured conditions for the unhampered and effective exercise of their rights and duties.

The immunity of Deputies, and other guarantees of their activity as Deputies, are defined in the Law on the Status of Deputies and other legislative acts of the USSR and of Union and Autonomous Republics.

Article 107. Deputies shall report on their work and on that of the Soviet to their constituents, and to the work collectives and public organisations that nominated them.

Deputies who have not justified the confidence of their constituents may be recalled at any time by decision of a majority of the electors in accordance with the procedure established by law.

V. Higher Bodies of State Authority and Administration of the USSR

Chapter 15: The Supreme Soviet of the USSR

Article 108. The highest body of state authority of the USSR shall be the Supreme Soviet of the USSR.

The Supreme Soviet of the USSR is empowered to deal with all matters within the jurisdiction of the Union of Soviet Socialist Republics, as defined by this Constitution.

The adoption and amendment of the Constitution of the USSR; admission of new Republics to the USSR; endorsement of the formation of new Autonomous Republics and Autonomous Regions; approval of the state plans for economic and social development, of the Budget of the USSR, and of reports on their execution; and the institution of bodies of the USSR accountable to it are the exclusive prerogative of the Supreme Soviet of the USSR.

Laws of the USSR shall be enacted by the Supreme Soviet of the USSR or by a nationwide vote (referendum) held by decision of the Supreme Soviet of the USSR.

Article 109. The Supreme Soviet of the USSR shall consist of two chambers: the Soviet of the Union and the Soviet of Nationalities.

The two chambers of the Supreme Soviet of the USSR shall have equal rights.

Article 110. The Soviet of the Union and the Soviet of Nationalities shall have equal numbers of deputies.

The Soviet of the Union shall be elected by constituencies with equal populations.

The Soviet of Nationalities shall be elected on the basis of the following representation: 32 deputies from each Union Republic, 11 deputies from each Autonomous Republic, five deputies from each Autonomous Region, and one deputy from each Autonomous Area.

The Soviet of the Union and the Soviet of Nationalities, upon submission by the credentials commissions elected by them, shall decide on the validity of Deputies' credentials, and, in cases in which the election law has been violated, shall declare the election of the Deputies concerned null and void.

Article 111. Each chamber of the Supreme Soviet of the USSR shall elect a Chairman and four Vice-Chairmen.

The Chairmen of the Soviet of the Union and of the Soviet of Nationalities shall preside over the sittings of the respective chambers and conduct their affairs.

Joint sittings of the chambers of the Supreme Soviet of the USSR shall be presided over alternately by the Chairman of the Soviet of the Union and the Chairman of the Soviet of Nationalities.

Article 112. Sessions of the Supreme Soviet of the USSR shall be convened twice a year.

Special sessions shall be convened by the Presidium of the Supreme Soviet of the USSR at its discretion or on the proposal of a Union Republic, or of not less than one-third of the Deputies of one of the chambers.

A session of the Supreme Soviet of the USSR shall consist of separate and joint sittings of the chambers, and of meetings of the standing commissions of the chambers or commissions of the Supreme Soviet of the USSR held between the sittings of the chambers. A session may be opened and closed at either separate or joint sittings of the chambers.

Article 113. The right to initiate legislation in the Supreme Soviet of the USSR is vested in the Soviet of the Union and the Soviet of Nationalities, the Presidium of the Supreme Soviet of the USSR, the Council of Ministers of the USSR, Union Republics through their highest bodies of state authority, commissions of the Supreme Soviet of the USSR and standing commissions of its chambers, Deputies of the Supreme Soviet of the USSR, the Supreme Court of the USSR, and the Procurator-General of the USSR.

The right to initiate legislation is also vested in public organisations through their All-Union bodies.

Article 114. Bills and other matters submitted to the Supreme Soviet of the USSR shall be debated by its chambers at separate or joint sittings. Where necessary, a bill or other matter may be referred to one or more commissions for preliminary or additional consideration.

A law of the USSR shall be deemed adopted when it has been

passed in each chamber of the Supreme Soviet of the USSR by a majority of the total number of its Deputies. Decisions and other acts of the Supreme Soviet of the USSR are adopted by a majority of the total number of Deputies of the Supreme Soviet of the USSR.

Bills and other very important matters of state may be submitted for nationwide discussion by a decision of the Supreme Soviet of the USSR or its Presidium taken on their own initiative or on the proposal of a Union Republic.

Article 115. In the event of disagreement between the Soviet of the Union and the Soviet of Nationalities, the matter at issue shall be referred for settlement to a conciliation commission formed by the chambers on a parity basis, after which it shall be considered for a second time by the Soviet of the Union and the Soviet of Nationalities at a joint sitting. If agreement is again not reached, the matter shall be postponed for debate at the next session of the Supreme Soviet of the USSR or submitted by the Supreme Soviet to a nationwide vote (referendum).

Article 116. Laws of the USSR and decisions and other acts of the Supreme Soviet of the USSR shall be published in the languages of the Union Republics over the signatures of the Chairman and Secretary of the Presidium of the Supreme Soviet of the USSR.

Article 117. A Deputy of the Supreme Soviet of the USSR has the right to address inquiries to the Council of Ministers of the USSR, and to Ministers and the heads of other bodies formed by the Supreme Soviet of the USSR. The Council of Ministers of the USSR, or the official to whom the inquiry is addressed, is obliged to give a verbal or written reply within three days at the given session of the Supreme Soviet of the USSR.

Article 118. A Deputy of the Supreme Soviet of the USSR may not be prosecuted, or arrested, or incur a court-imposed penalty, without the sanction of the Supreme Soviet of the USSR or, between its sessions, of the Presidium of the Supreme Soviet of the USSR.

Article 119. The Supreme Soviet of the USSR, at a joint sitting of its chambers, shall elect a Presidium of the Supreme Soviet of the USSR, which shall be a standing body of the Supreme Soviet of the USSR, accountable to it for all its work and exercising the functions of the highest body of state authority of the USSR between sessions of the Supreme Soviet, within the limits prescribed by the Constitution.

Article 120. The Presidium of the Supreme Soviet of the USSR shall be elected from among the Deputies and shall consist of a Chairman, First Vice-Chairman, 15 Vice-Chairmen (one from each Union Republic), a Secretary, and 21 members.

Article 121. The Presidium of the Supreme Soviet of the USSR shall:

1. name the date of elections to the Supreme Soviet of the USSR;
2. convene sessions of the Supreme Soviet of the USSR;
3. co-ordinate the work of the standing commissions of the chambers of the Supreme Soviet of the USSR;
4. ensure observance of the Constitution of the USSR and conformity of the Constitutions and laws of Union Republics to the Constitution and laws of the USSR;
5. interpret the laws of the USSR;
6. ratify and denounce international treaties of the USSR;
7. revoke decisions and ordinances of the Council of Ministers of the USSR and of the Councils of Ministers of Union Republics should they fail to conform to the law;
8. institute military and diplomatic ranks and other special titles; and confer the highest military and diplomatic ranks and other special titles;
9. institute orders and medals of the USSR, and honorific titles of the USSR; award orders and medals of the USSR; and confer honorific titles of the USSR;
10. grant citizenship of the USSR, and rule on matters of the renunciation or deprivation of citizenship of the USSR and of granting asylum;
11. issue All-Union acts of amnesty and exercise the right of pardon;
12. appoint and recall diplomatic representatives of the USSR to other countries and to international organisations;
13. receive the letters of credence and recall of the diplomatic representatives of foreign states accredited to it;
14. form the Council of Defence of the USSR and confirm its composition; appoint and dismiss the high command of the Armed Forces of the USSR;
15. proclaim martial law in particular localities or throughout the country in the interests of defence of the USSR;
16. order general or partial mobilisation;
17. between sessions of the Supreme Soviet of the USSR, proclaim a state of war in the event of an armed attack on the USSR,

or when it is necessary to meet international treaty obligations relating to mutual defence against aggression;

18. and exercise other powers vested in it by the Constitution and laws of the USSR.

Article 122. The Presidium of the Supreme Soviet of the USSR, between sessions of the Supreme Soviet of the USSR and subject to submission for its confirmation at the next session, shall:

1. amend existing legislative acts of the USSR when necessary;
2. approve changes in the boundaries between Union Republics;
3. form and abolish Ministries and State Committees of the USSR on the recommendation of the Council of Ministers of the USSR;
4. relieve individual members of the Council of Ministers of the USSR of their responsibilities and appoint persons to the Council of Ministers on the recommendation of the Chairman of the Council of Ministers of the USSR.

Article 123. The Presidium of the Supreme Soviet of the USSR promulgates decrees and adopts decisions.

Article 124. On expiry of the term of the Supreme Soviet of the USSR, the Presidium of the Supreme Soviet of the USSR shall retain its powers until the newly elected Supreme Soviet of the USSR has elected a new Presidium.

The newly elected Supreme Soviet of the USSR shall be convened by the outgoing Presidium of the Supreme Soviet of the USSR within two months of the elections.

Article 125. The Soviet of the Union and the Soviet of Nationalities shall elect standing commissions from among the Deputies to make a preliminary review of matters coming within the jurisdiction of the Supreme Soviet of the USSR, to promote execution of the laws of the USSR and other acts of the Supreme Soviet of the USSR and its Presidium, and to check on the work of state bodies and organisations. The chambers of the Supreme Soviet of the USSR may also set up joint commissions on a parity basis.

When it deems it necessary, the Supreme Soviet of the USSR sets up commissions of inquiry and audit, and commissions on any other matter.

All state and public bodies, organisations and officials are obliged to meet the requests of the commissions of the Supreme Soviet of the USSR and of its chambers, and submit the requisite materials and documents to them.

The commissions' recommendations shall be subject to consideration by state and public bodies, institutions and organisations. The commissions shall be informed, within the prescribed time-limit, of the results of such consideration or of the action taken.

Article 126. The Supreme Soviet of the USSR shall supervise the work of all state bodies accountable to it.

The Supreme Soviet of the USSR shall form a Committee of People's Control of the USSR to head the system of people's control.

The organisation and procedure of people's control bodies are defined by the Law on People's Control in the USSR.

Article 127. The procedure of the Supreme Soviet of the USSR and of its bodies shall be defined in the Rules and Regulations of the Supreme Soviet of the USSR and other laws of the USSR enacted on the basis of the Constitution of the USSR.

Chapter 16: The Council of Ministers of the USSR

Article 128. The Council of Ministers of the USSR, i.e. the Government of the USSR, is the highest executive and administrative body of state authority of the USSR.

Article 129. The Council of Ministers of the USSR shall be formed by the Supreme Soviet of the USSR at a joint sitting of the Soviet of the Union and the Soviet of Nationalities, and shall consist of the Chairman of the Council of Ministers of the USSR, First Vice-Chairmen and Vice-Chairmen, Ministers of the USSR, and Chairmen of State Committees of the USSR.

The Chairmen of the Councils of Ministers of Union Republics shall be *ex officio* members of the Council of Ministers of the USSR.

The Supreme Soviet of the USSR, on the recommendation of the Chairman of the Council of Ministers of the USSR, may include in the Government of the USSR the heads of other bodies and organisations of the USSR.

The Council of Ministers of the USSR shall tender its resignation to a newly elected Supreme Soviet of the USSR at its first session.

Article 130. The Council of Ministers of the USSR shall be responsible and accountable to the Supreme Soviet of the USSR and, between sessions of the Supreme Soviet of the USSR, to the Presidium of the Supreme Soviet of the USSR.

The Council of Ministers of the USSR shall report regularly on its work to the Supreme Soviet of the USSR.

Article 131. The Council of Ministers of the USSR is empowered to deal with all matters of state administration within the jurisdiction of the Union of Soviet Socialist Republics insofar as, under the Constitution, they do not come within the competence of the Supreme Soviet of the USSR or the Presidium of the Supreme Soviet of the USSR.

Within its powers the Council of Ministers of the USSR shall:

1. ensure direction of economic, social, and cultural development; draft and implement measures to promote the well-being and cultural development of the people, to develop science and engineering, to ensure rational exploitation and conservation of natural resources, to consolidate the monetary and credit system, to pursue a uniform prices, wages, and social security policy, and to organise state insurance and a uniform system of accounting and statistics; and organise the management of industrial, constructional, and agricultural enterprises and amalgamations, transport and communications undertakings, banks, and other organisations and institutions of All-Union subordination;

2. draft current and long-term state plans for the economic and social development of the USSR and the Budget of the USSR, and submit them to the Supreme Soviet of the USSR; take measures to execute the state plans and Budget; and report to the Supreme Soviet of the USSR on the implementation of the plans and Budget;

3. implement measures to defend the interests of the state, protect socialist property and maintain public order, and guarantee and protect citizens' rights and freedoms;

4. take measures to ensure state security;

5. exercise general direction of the development of the Armed Forces of the USSR, and determine the annual contingent of citizens to be called up for active military service;

6. provide general direction in regard to relations with other states, foreign trade, and economic, scientific, technical, and cultural co-operation of the USSR with other countries; take measures to ensure fulfilment of the USSR's international treaties; and ratify and denounce intergovernmental international agreements;

7. and when necessary, form committees, central boards and other departments under the Council of Ministers of the USSR to deal with matters of economic, social and cultural development, and defence.

Article 132. A Presidium of the Council of Ministers of the

USSR, consisting of the Chairman, the First Vice-Chairmen, and Vice-Chairmen of the Council of Ministers of the USSR, shall function as a standing body of the Council of Ministers of the USSR to deal with questions relating to guidance of the economy, and with other matters of state administration.

Article 133. The Council of Ministers of the USSR, on the basis of, and in pursuance of, the laws of the USSR and other decisions of the Supreme Soviet of the USSR and its Presidium, shall issue decisions and ordinances and verify their execution. The decisions and ordinances of the Council of Ministers of the USSR shall be binding throughout the USSR.

Article 134. The Council of Ministers of the USSR has the right, in matters within the jurisdiction of the Union of Soviet Socialist Republics, to suspend execution of decisions and ordinances of the Councils of Ministers of Union Republics, and to rescind acts of ministries and state committees of the USSR, and of other bodies subordinate to it.

Article 135. The Council of Ministers of the USSR shall coordinate and direct the work of All-Union and Union-Republican ministries, state committees of the USSR, and other bodies subordinate to it.

All-Union ministries and state committees of the USSR shall direct the work of the branches of administration entrusted to them, or exercise inter-branch administration, throughout the territory of the USSR directly or through bodies set up by them.

Union-Republican ministries and state committees of the USSR direct the work of the branches of administration entrusted to them, or exercise inter-branch administration, as a rule, through the corresponding ministries and state committees, and other bodies of Union Republics, and directly administer individual enterprises and amalgamations of Union subordination. The procedure for transferring enterprises and amalgamations from Republic or local subordination to Union subordination shall be defined by the Presidium of the Supreme Soviet of the USSR.

Ministries and state committees of the USSR shall be responsible for the condition and development of the spheres of administration entrusted to them; within their competence, they issue orders and other acts on the basis of, and in execution of, the laws of the USSR and other decisions of the Supreme Soviet of the USSR and its Presidium, and of decisions and ordinances of the Council of Ministers of the USSR, and organise and verify their implementation.

Article 136. The competence of the Council of Ministers of the USSR and its Presidium, the procedure for their work, relationships between the Council of Ministers and other state bodies, and the list of All-Union and Union-Republican ministries and state committees of the USSR are defined, on the basis of the Constitution, in the Law on the Council of Ministers of the USSR.

VI. Basic Principles of the Structure of the Bodies of State Authority and Administration in Union Republics

Chapter 17: Higher Bodies of State Authority and Administration of a Union Republic

Article 137. The highest body of state authority of a Union Republic shall be the Supreme Soviet of that Republic.

The Supreme Soviet of a Union Republic is empowered to deal with all matters within the jurisdiction of the Republic under the Constitutions of the USSR and the Republic.

Adoption and amendment of the Constitution of a Union Republic; endorsement of state plans for economic and social development, of the Republic's Budget, and of reports on their fulfilment; and the formation of bodies accountable to the Supreme Soviet of the Union Republic are the exclusive prerogative of that Supreme Soviet.

Laws of a Union Republic shall be enacted by the Supreme Soviet of the Union Republic or by a popular vote (referendum) held by decision of the Republic's Supreme Soviet.

Article 138. The Supreme Soviet of a Union Republic shall elect a Presidium, which is a standing body of that Supreme Soviet and accountable to it for all its work. The composition and powers of the Presidium of the Supreme Soviet of a Union Republic shall be defined in the Constitution of the Union Republic.

Article 139. The Supreme Soviet of a Union Republic shall form a Council of Ministers of the Union Republic, i.e. the Government of that Republic, which shall be the highest executive and administrative body of state authority in the Republic.

The Council of Ministers of a Union Republic shall be responsible and accountable to the Supreme Soviet of that Republic or, between sessions of the Supreme Soviet, to its Presidium.

Article 140. The Council of Ministers of a Union Republic issues decisions and ordinances on the basis of, and in pursuance of, the legislative acts of the USSR and of the Union Republic, and of decisions and ordinances of the Council of Ministers of the USSR, and shall organise and verify their execution.

Article 141. The Council of Ministers of a Union Republic has the right to suspend the execution of decisions and ordinances of the Councils of Ministers of Autonomous Republics, to rescind the decisions and orders of the Executive Committees of Soviets of People's Deputies of Territories, Regions, and cities (i.e. cities under Republic jurisdiction) and of Autonomous Regions, and in Union Republics not divided into regions, of the Executive Committees of district and corresponding city Soviets of People's Deputies.

Article 142. The Council of Ministers of a Union Republic shall co-ordinate and direct the work of the Union-Republican and Republican ministries and of state committees of the Union Republic, and other bodies under its jurisdiction.

The Union-Republican ministries and state committees of a Union Republic shall direct the branches of administration entrusted to them, or exercise inter-branch control, and shall be subordinate to both the Council of Ministers of the Union Republic and the corresponding Union-Republican ministry or state committee of the USSR.

Republican ministries and state committees shall direct the branches of administration entrusted to them, or exercise inter-branch control, and shall be subordinate to the Council of Ministers of the Union Republic.

Chapter 18: Higher Bodies of State Authority and Administration of an Autonomous Republic

Article 143. The highest body of state authority of an Autonomous Republic shall be the Supreme Soviet of that Republic.

Adoption and amendment of the Constitution of an Autonomous Republic; endorsement of state plans for economic and social development, and of the Republic's Budget; and the formation of bodies accountable to the Supreme Soviet of the Autonomous Republic are the exclusive prerogative of that Supreme Soviet.

Laws of an Autonomous Republic shall be enacted by the Supreme Soviet of the Autonomous Republic.

Article 144. The Supreme Soviet of an Autonomous Republic shall elect a Presidium of the Supreme Soviet of the Autonomous Republic and shall form a Council of Ministers of the Autonomous Republic, i.e., the Government of that Republic.

Chapter 19: Local Bodies of State Authority and Administration

Article 145. The bodies of state authority in Territories, Regions, Autonomous Regions, Autonomous Areas, districts, cities, city districts, settlements, and rural communities shall be the corresponding Soviets of People's Deputies.

Article 146. Local Soviets of People's Deputies shall deal with all matters of local significance in accordance with the interests of the whole state and of the citizens residing in the area under their jurisdiction, implement decisions of higher bodies of state authority, guide the work of lower Soviets of People's Deputies, take part in the discussion of matters of Republican and All-Union significance, and submit their proposals concerning them.

Local Soviets of People's Deputies shall direct state, economic, social and cultural development within their territory; endorse plans for economic and social development and the local budget; exercise general guidance over state bodies, enterprises, institutions and organisations subordinate to them; ensure observance of the laws, maintenance of law and order, and protection of citizens' rights; and help strengthen the country's defence capacity.

Article 147. Within their powers, local Soviets of People's Deputies shall ensure the comprehensive, all-round economic and social development of their area; exercise control over the observance of legislation by enterprises, institutions and organisations subordinate to higher authorities and located in their area; and coordinate and supervise their activity as regards land use, nature conservation, building, employment of manpower, production of consumer goods, and social, cultural, communal and other services and amenities for the public.

Article 148. Local Soviets of People's Deputies shall decide matters within the powers accorded them by the legislation of the

USSR and of the appropriate Union Republic and Autonomous Republic. Their decisions shall be binding on all enterprises, institutions, and organisations located in their area and on officials and citizens.

Article 149. The executive-administrative bodies of local Soviets shall be the Executive Committees elected by them from among their deputies.

Executive Committees shall report on their work at least once a year to the Soviets that elected them and to meetings of citizens at their places of work or residence.

Article 150. Executive Committees of local Soviets of People's Deputies shall be directly accountable both to the Soviet that elected them and to the higher executive and administrative body.

VII. Justice, Arbitration, and Procurator's Supervision

Chapter 20: Courts and Arbitration

Article 151. In the USSR justice is administered only by the courts.

In the USSR there are the following courts: the Supreme Court of the USSR, the Supreme Courts of Union Republics, the Supreme Courts of Autonomous Republics, Territorial, Regional, and city courts, courts of Autonomous Regions, courts of Autonomous Areas, district (city) people's courts, and military tribunals in the Armed Forces.

Article 152. All courts in the USSR shall be formed on the principle of the electiveness of judges and people's assessors.

People's judges of district (city) people's courts shall be elected for a term of five years by the citizens of the district (city) on the basis of universal, equal and direct suffrage by secret ballot. People's assessors of district (city) people's courts shall be elected for a term of two and a half years at meetings of citizens at their places of work or residence by a show of hands.

Higher courts shall be elected for a term of five years by the corresponding Soviet of People's Deputies.

The judges of military tribunals shall be elected for a term of five years by the Presidium of the Supreme Soviet of the USSR and people's assessors for a term of two and a half years by meetings of servicemen.

Judges and people's assessors are responsible and accountable to their electors or the bodies that elected them, shall report to them, and may be recalled by them in the manner prescribed by law.

Article 153. The Supreme Court of the USSR is the highest judicial body in the USSR and supervises the administration of justice by the courts of the USSR and Union Republics within the limits established by law.

The Supreme Court of the USSR shall be elected by the Supreme Soviet of the USSR and shall consist of a Chairman, Vice-Chairmen, members, and people's assessors. The Chairmen of the Supreme Courts of Union Republics are *ex officio* members of the Supreme Court of the USSR.

The organisation and procedure of the Supreme Court of the USSR are defined in the Law on the Supreme Court of the USSR.

Article 154. The hearing of civil and criminal cases in all courts is collegial; in courts of first instance cases are heard with the participation of people's assessors. In the administration of justice people's assessors have all the rights of a judge.

Article 155. Judges and people's assessors are independent and subject only to the law.

Article 156. Justice is administered in the USSR on the principle of the equality of citizens before the law and the court.

Article 157. Proceedings in all courts shall be open to the public. Hearings *in camera* are only allowed in cases provided for by law, with observance of all the rules of judicial procedure.

Article 158. A defendant in a criminal action is guaranteed the right to legal assistance.

Article 159. Judicial proceedings shall be conducted in the language of the Union Republic, Autonomous Republic, Autonomous Region, or Autonomous Area, or in the language spoken by the majority of the people in the locality. Persons participating in court proceedings, who do not know the language in which they are being conducted, shall be ensured the right to become fully acquainted with the materials in the case; the services of an interpreter during the proceedings; and the right to address the court in their own language.

Article 160. No one may be adjudged guilty of a crime and subjected to punishment as a criminal except by the sentence of a court and in conformity with the law.

Article 161. Colleges of advocates are available to give legal assistance to citizens and organisations. In cases provided for by legislation citizens shall be given legal assistance free of charge.

The organisation and procedure of the bar are determined by legislation of the USSR and Union Republics.

Article 162. Representatives of public organisations and of work collectives may take part in civil and criminal proceedings.

Article 163. Economic disputes between enterprises, institutions, and organisations are settled by state arbitration bodies within the limits of their jurisdiction.

The organisation and manner of functioning of state arbitration bodies are defined in the Law on State Arbitration in the USSR.

Chapter 21: The Procurator's Office

Article 164. Supreme power of supervision over the strict and uniform observance of laws by all ministries, state committees and departments, enterprises, institutions and organisations, executive-administrative bodies of local Soviets of People's Deputies, collective farms, co-operatives and other public organisations, officials and citizens is vested in the Procurator-General of the USSR and procurators subordinate to him.

Article 165. The Procurator-General of the USSR is appointed by the Supreme Soviet of the USSR and is responsible and accountable to it and, between sessions of the Supreme Soviet, to the Presidium of the Supreme Soviet of the USSR.

Article 166. The procurators of Union Republics, Autonomous Republics, Territories, Regions and Autonomous Regions are appointed by the Procurator-General of the USSR. The procurators of Autonomous Areas and district and city procurators are appointed by the Procurators of Union Republics, subject to confirmation by the Procurator-General of the USSR.

Article 167. The term of office of the Procurator-General of the USSR and all lower-ranking procurators shall be five years.

Article 168. The agencies of the Procurator's Office exercise their powers independently of any local bodies whatsoever, and are subordinate solely to the Procurator-General of the USSR.

The organisation and procedure of the agencies of the Procurator's Office are defined in the Law on the Procurator's Office of the USSR.

VIII. The Emblem, Flag, Anthem, and Capital of the USSR

Article 169. The State Emblem of the Union of Soviet Socialist Republics is a hammer and sickle on a globe depicted in the rays of the sun and framed by ears of wheat, with the inscription "Workers of All Countries, Unite!" in the languages of the Union Republics. At the top of the Emblem is a five-pointed star.

Article 170. The State Flag of the Union of Soviet Socialist Republics is a rectangle of red cloth with a hammer and sickle depicted in gold in the upper corner next to the staff and with a five-pointed red star edged in gold above them. The ratio of the width of the flag to its length is 1:2.

Article 171. The State Anthem of the Union of Soviet Socialist Republics is confirmed by the Presidium of the Supreme Soviet of the USSR.

Article 172. The Capital of the Union of Soviet Socialist Republics is the city of Moscow.

IX. The Legal Force of the Constitution of the USSR and Procedure for Amending the Constitution

Article 173. The Constitution of the USSR shall have supreme legal force. All laws and other acts of state bodies shall be promulgated on the basis of and in conformity with it.

Article 174. The Constitution of the USSR may be amended by a decision of the Supreme Soviet of the USSR adopted by a majority of not less than two-thirds of the total number of Deputies of each of its chambers.

Workers of all countries, unite!

Appendix 3: Rules of the Communist Party of the Soviet Union

(with amendments and additions introduced with account of the proposals received in the course of the Party-wide discussion)

THE COMMUNIST PARTY of the Soviet Union is the tried and tested militant vanguard of the Soviet people, which unites, on a voluntary basis, the more advanced, politically more conscious section of the working class, collective-farm peasantry and intelligentsia of the USSR.

Founded by V. I. Lenin as the vanguard of the working class, the Communist Party has travelled a glorious road of struggle, and brought the working class and the working peasantry to the victory of the Great October Socialist Revolution and to the establishment of the dictatorship of the proletariat in our country. Under the leadership of the Communist Party, the exploiting classes were abolished in the Soviet Union, and the socio-political and ideological unity of multinational Soviet society has taken shape and is steadily growing in strength. Socialism has triumphed completely and finally. The proletarian state has grown into a state of the entire people. The country has entered the stage of developed socialism.

The CPSU, remaining, in its class essence and ideology, a Party of the working class, has become the Party of the entire people.

The Party exists for, and serves, the people. It is the highest form of socio-political organization, the nucleus of the political system and the leading and guiding force of Soviet society. The Party defines the general perspective in the development of the country,

---

From Supplement to *Moscow News*, no. 11 (3707), 1986.

secures the scientific guidance of the people's creative activities, and imparts an organized, planned and purposeful character to their struggle to achieve the ultimate goal, the victory of communism.

In all its activities, the CPSU takes guidance from Marxist-Leninist teachings and its own Programme, which defines the tasks of the planned and all-round perfection of socialism and of the further progress of Soviet society towards communism on the basis of the acceleration of the country's socio-economic development.

The CPSU bases its work on unswerving adherence to the Leninist standards of Party life, the principles of democratic centralism, of collective leadership, the promotion, in every possible way, of inner-Party democracy, creative activity of the Communists, criticism and self-criticism and broad publicity.

Ideological and organizational unity, monolithic cohesion of its ranks, and a high degree of conscious discipline on the part of all Communists are an inviolable law of the CPSU. All manifestations of factionalism and group activity are incompatible with Marxist-Leninist Party principles, and with Party membership. The Party expels persons who violate the Programme and the Rules of the CPSU and compromise the lofty name of Communist by their behaviour.

In creatively developing Marxism-Leninism, the CPSU vigorously combats all manifestations of revisionism and dogmatism, which are utterly alien to revolutionary theory.

The Communist Party of the Soviet Union is an integral part of the international communist movement. It firmly adheres to the tried and tested Marxist-Leninist principles of proletarian, socialist internationalism, actively promotes the strengthening of cooperation and cohesion of the fraternal socialist countries, the world system of socialism, the international communist and working class movement, and expresses solidarity with the nations waging a struggle for national and social liberation, against imperialism and for the preservation of peace.

I. Party Members, Their Duties and Rights

1. Membership of the CPSU is open to any citizen of the Soviet Union who accepts the Programme and the Rules of the Party, takes an active part in communist construction, works in one of the

Party organizations, carries out all Party decisions, and pays membership dues.

2. It is the duty of a Party member:

(a) to implement, firmly and undeviatingly, the Party's general line and directives, to explain to the masses the CPSU's internal and foreign policy, to organize the working people for its implementation, and to promote the strengthening and expansion of the Party's ties with the people;

(b) to set an example in labour, to protect and increase socialist property, to work persistently for raising production efficiency, for a steady growth of labour productivity, for improving the quality of output, for the application of modern achievements in science and technology and advanced know-how in the country's economy; to perfect his own qualifications, to be an active adherent to everything new and progressive, to make the utmost contribution to accelerating the country's socio-economic development;

(c) to be active in the country's political life, in the administration of state and public affairs, to set an example in the fulfilment of civic duty, to promote actively the ever fuller implementation of the people's socialist self-government;

(d) to master Marxist-Leninist theory, to expand his political and cultural field of vision, and promote in all possible ways the growth of the Soviet people's consciousness and their ideological-moral growth. To wage a resolute struggle against any manifestations of bourgeois ideology, private-property psychology, religious prejudices and other views and morals alien to the socialist way of life;

(e) to abide strictly by the norms of communist morality, to assert the principle of social justice which is innate in socialism, to put public interests above personal, to display modesty and decency, responsiveness and attentiveness to people, to respond promptly to working people's requirements and needs; to be truthful and honest with the Party and the people;

(f) to propagate consistently the ideas of proletarian, socialist internationalism and Soviet patriotism among the masses of the working people, to combat manifestations of nationalism and chauvinism, to promote actively the strengthening of friendship of the USSR peoples and fraternal relations with the countries of socialism, with the proletarians and working people of the whole world;

(g) to help, in every possible way, to strengthen the defence capacity of the USSR, to wage an unflagging struggle for peace and friendship among nations;

(h) to strengthen the ideological and organizational unity of the Party, to safeguard the Party against the infiltration of people unworthy of the lofty name of Communist, to display vigilance, to guard Party and state secrets;

(i) to develop criticism and self-criticism, boldly lay bare shortcomings and strive for their removal, to combat ostentation, conceit, complacency and eyewash, to rebuff firmly all attempts at suppressing criticism, to resist red tape, parochialism, departmentalism and all actions injurious to the Party and the state and to give information of them to Party bodies, up to and including the CC CPSU;

(j) to implement undeviatingly the Party's policy with regard to the proper selection of personnel according to their political and professional qualifications and moral qualities. To be uncompromising whenever the Leninist principles of the selection and education of personnel are infringed;

(k) to observe Party and state discipline, which is equally binding on all Party members. The Party has one discipline, one law, for all Communists, irrespective of their past services or the positions they occupy.

3. A Party member has the right:

(a) to elect and be elected to Party bodies;

(b) to discuss freely questions of the Party's policies and practical activities at Party meetings, conferences and congresses, at the meetings of Party committees and in the Party press; to table motions; openly to express and uphold his opinion as long as the Party organization concerned has not adopted a decision;

(c) to criticize any Party organ and any Communist, irrespective of the position he holds, at Party meetings, conferences and congresses, and at the plenary meetings of Party committees. Those who commit the offence of suppressing criticism or victimizing anyone for criticism are responsible to and will be penalized by the Party, to the point of expulsion from the CPSU;

(d) to attend in person all Party meetings and all bureau and committee meetings that discuss his activities or conduct;

(e) to address any question, statement or proposal to any Party body, up to and including the CC CPSU, and to demand an answer on the substance of his address.

4. Applicants are admitted to Party membership only individually. Membership of the Party is open to politically conscious and active citizens from among workers, peasants and intellectuals devoted to the communist cause. New members are admitted from

among the candidate members who have passed through the established probationary period.

Persons may join the Party on attaining the age of 18. Young people up to the age of 25 may join the Party only through the Leninist Young Communist League of the Soviet Union (YCL).

The procedure for the admission of candidate members to full Party membership is as follows:

(a) Applicants for Party membership must submit recommendations from three members of the CPSU who have a Party standing of not less than five years and who know the applicants from having worked with them, professionally and socially, for not less than one year.

Note 1. In the case of members of the YCL applying for membership of the Party, the recommendation of a district or city committee of the YCL is equivalent to the recommendation of one Party member.

Note 2. Members and alternate members of the CPSU Central Committee shall refrain from giving recommendations.

(b) Applications for Party membership are discussed and a decision is taken by the general meeting of the primary Party organization; the decision of the latter is considered accepted if not less than two-thirds of the Party members present at the meeting have voted for it, and takes effect after endorsement by the district Party committee, or by the city Party committee in cities with no district division.

The question of admittance to the Party may be discussed without the presence of those who have recommended an applicant for Party membership. Admittance to the Party is done, as a rule, at open meetings;

(c) citizens of the USSR who formerly belonged to the Communist or Workers' Party of another country, are admitted to membership of the Communist Party of the Soviet Union in conformity with the rules established by the CPSU Central Committee.

5. Communists recommending applicants for Party membership are responsible to Party organizations for the impartiality of their description of the political and professional qualifications and moral qualities of those they recommended and help them to perfect their ideological and political knowledge.

6. The Party standing of those admitted to Party membership dates from the day when the general meeting of the primary Party organization decides to accept them as full members.

7. The procedure of registering members and candidate mem-

bers of the Party, and their transfer from one organization to another is determined by the appropriate instructions of the CC CPSU.

8. If a Party member or candidate member fails to pay membership dues for three months in succession without sufficient reason, the matter shall be discussed by the primary Party organization. If it is revealed as a result that the Party member or candidate member in question has virtually lost contact with the Party organization, he shall be regarded as having ceased to be a member of the Party; the primary Party organization shall pass a decision thereon and submit it to the district or city committee of the Party for endorsement.

9. A Party member or candidate member who fails to fulfil his duties as laid down in the Rules, or commits other offences, shall be called to account, and may be subjected to the penalty of admonition, reprimand (severe reprimand), or reprimand (severe reprimand) with entry in the registration card. The highest Party penalty is expulsion from the Party.

In the case of significant offences, measures of Party education and influence should be applied in the form of comradely criticism, Party censure, warning or reproof.

A Communist who has committed an offence must answer for it, above all, to his primary Party organization. In the event of a Communist being called to account before the Party by a superior organ, the primary Party organization will be informed about this.

When the question of calling a Party member to account before the Party is discussed the maximum attention must be shown and the grounds for the charges preferred against him must be thoroughly investigated.

The Party organization gives the Party member a hearing, no later than a year after the penalty was imposed on him, to find out how he is rectifying his shortcomings.

10. The question of expelling a Communist from the Party is decided by the general meeting of a primary Party organization. The decision of the primary Party organization expelling a member is regarded as adopted if not less than two-thirds of the Party members attending the meeting have voted for it, and takes effect after endorsement by the district or city Party committee.

Until such time as the decision to expel him is endorsed by the district or city Party committee, the Party member or candidate member retains his membership card and is entitled to attend closed Party meetings.

An expelled Party member retains the right to appeal, within the period of two months, to the higher Party bodies up to and including the CC CPSU.

11. The question of calling a member or alternate member of the CC of the Communist Party of a Union Republic, of a territorial, regional, area, city or district Party committee, as well as a member of an auditing commission, to account before the Party is discussed by primary Party organizations; and decisions imposing penalties on them are taken in accordance with the regular procedure.

A Party organization which proposes expelling a Communist from the CPSU communicates its proposal to the Party committee of which he is a member. A decision expelling from the Party a member or alternate member of the CC of the Communist Party of a Union Republic or a territorial, regional, area, city or district Party committee, or a member of an auditing commission, is taken at the plenary meeting of the committee concerned by a majority of two-thirds of the membership.

The decision to expel from the Party a member or alternate member of the Central Committee of the CPSU, or a member of the Central Auditing Commission of the CPSU, is made by the Party Congress, and in the interim between two congresses, by a plenary meeting of the Central Committee, by a majority of two-thirds of its members.

12. A Party member bears a double responsibility for the infringement of Soviet laws—to the state and the Party. Persons who have committed indictable offences are expelled from the CPSU.

13. Appeals against the expulsion from the Party or against the imposition of a penalty, as well as the decisions of Party organizations on expulsion from the Party, shall be examined by the appropriate Party bodies within not more than two months from the date of their receipt.

II. Candidate Members

14. All persons joining the Party must pass through a probationary period as candidate members in order to more thoroughly familiarize themselves with the Programme and the Rules of the CPSU and prepare for admission to full membership of the Party. Party organizations must assist candidates to prepare for admission to full membership of the Party, and test their personal qualities in practical deeds, in fulfilment of Party and public assignments.

The period of probationary membership is one year.

15. The procedure for the admission of candidate members (individual admission, submission of recommendations, decision of the primary organization as to admission, and its endorsement) is identical with the procedure for the admission of Party members.

16. On the expiration of a candidate member's probationary period the primary Party organization discusses and passes a decision on his admission to full membership. Should a candidate member fail, in the course of his probationary period, to prove his worthiness, and should his personal traits make it evident that he cannot be admitted to membership of the CPSU, the Party organization shall pass a decision rejecting his admission to membership of the Party; after endorsement of that decision by the district or city Party committee, he shall cease to be considered a candidate member of the CPSU.

17. Candidate members of the Party participate in all the activities of their Party organizations; they shall have a consultative voice at Party meetings. They may not be elected to any leading Party body, nor may they be elected delegates to a Party conference or congress.

18. Candidate members of the CPSU pay membership dues at the same rate as full members.

III. Organizational Structure of the Party. Inner-Party Democracy

19. The guiding principle of the organizational structure, of the entire life and activities of the Party is democratic centralism, which signifies

(a) election of all leading Party bodies, from the lowest to the highest;

(b) periodical reports of Party bodies to their Party organizations and to higher bodies;

(c) strict Party discipline and subordination of the minority to the majority;

(d) the decisions of higher bodies are obligatory for lower bodies;

(e) teamship in the work of all organizations and leading bodies of the Party and personal responsibility of every Communist for the fulfilment of his duties and Party assignments.

20. The Party is built on the territorial-and-production principle: primary organizations are established wherever Communists are employed, and are associated territorially in district, city and other organizations. An organization uniting the Communists of a given area is higher than any component Party organization of that area.

21. All Party organizations are autonomous in the decision of local questions, unless their decisions conflict with Party policy.

22. The highest leading body of a Party organization is the general meeting or conference (in the case of primary organizations), conference (in the case of district, city, area, regional or territorial organizations), or Congress (in the case of the Communist Parties of the Union Republics and the Communist Party of the Soviet Union). A meeting, conference or Congress are considered competent if they are attended by more than one half of the members of the Party organization or of the elected delegates.

23. The general meeting, conference or Congress elects a bureau or committee which acts as its executive body and directs all the current work of the Party organization.

An apparatus is being set up at the CC CPSU, the CCs of the Communist Parties of the Union Republics, territorial, regional area, city and district Party committees, for doing current work on the organization and checking up on the fulfilment of Party decisions and rendering assistance to the lower organizations in their activities.

The CPSU Central Committee defines the structure and the staff of the apparatus.

24. The election of Party bodies is effected by secret ballot. Elections of the secretaries, deputy secretaries of Party organizations and Party group organizers at meetings of primary, shop or departmental organizations with less than 15 Party members and of Party groups may be held, with the consent of the Communists, by a show of hands vote. In these primary organizations the elections of delegates to district and city Party conferences are held in the same order.

In an election, all Party members have the unlimited right to challenge candidates and to criticize them. Each candidate shall be voted upon separately. A candidate is considered elected if more than one half of those attending the meeting, conference or Congress have voted for him.

The principle of systematic renewal of the composition of Party bodies and of continuity of leadership shall be observed in the election of all Party organs—from primary organizations to the CPSU Central Committee.

25. A member or alternate member of the CC CPSU, CC of the Communist Party of a Union Republic, a territorial, regional, area, city or district Party committee must by his entire activity justify the great trust placed in him by the Party. A member or alternate member of the Party committee who degrades his honour and dignity may not remain on it.

The question of the removal of a member or an alternate member of a Party committee from that body is decided by a plenary meeting of the given committee. The decision is regarded as adopted if not less than two-thirds of the members of the Party committee vote for it by secret ballot.

The question of the removal of a member of the CPSU Central Auditing Commission, or of the auditing commission of a local Party organization from this commission is decided at its meetings according to the procedure envisaged for the members and alternate members of Party committees.

26. The free and businesslike discussion of questions of Party policy in the Party, in all of its organizations is an important principle of inner-Party democracy. Only on the basis of inner-Party democracy is it possible to ensure Communists' high creative activity, open criticism and self-criticism, and strong Party discipline, which must be conscious and not mechanical.

Discussion of controversial or insufficiently clear issues may be held within the framework of individual organizations or the Party as a whole.

Party-wide discussion is held:

(a) at the initiative of the CC CPSU if it considers it necessary to consult the Party as a whole on any particular question of policy;

(b) on the proposal of several Party organizations at Republican, territorial or regional level.

Wide discussion, especially discussion on a countrywide scale, of questions of Party policy must be so held as to ensure for Party members the free expression of their views and preclude attempts to form factional groupings and to split the Party.

27. The supreme principle of Party leadership is collective leadership, which is an absolute requisite for the normal functioning of Party organizations, the proper education of cadres, and the pro-

motion of the activity and initiative of Communists, and a reliable guarantee against the adoption of volitional, subjectivist decisions, manifestation of the cult of the individual and violations of Leninist norms of Party life.

Collective leadership presupposes personal responsibility for the assigned job and permanent control over the activity of every Party organization and every worker.

28. The CC CPSU, the Central Committees of the Communist Parties of the Union Republics, and territorial, regional, area, city and district Party committees shall systematically inform Party organizations of their work in the interim between congresses and conferences, and of the realization of the critical remarks and proposals made by Communists.

Objective and timely information of the higher Party bodies of their activities and the state of things in the localities must also be the hard and fast rule for Party committees and primary Party organizations.

29. Meetings of the active of district, city, area, regional and territorial Party organizations and of the Communist Parties of the Union Republics shall be held to discuss major decisions of the Party and to work out measures for their execution, as well as to examine questions of local significance.

30. Standing or temporary commissions and working groups on different questions of Party work may be set up at the Party committees, and other forms can also be used to draw Communists into the activities of the Party organs on a voluntary basis.

IV. Higher Party Organs

31. The supreme organ of the Communist Party of the Soviet Union is the Party Congress. Congresses are convened by the Central Committee at least once in five years. The convocation of a Party Congress and its agenda shall be announced at least six weeks before the Congress.

Extraordinary Congresses are convened by the Central Committee of the Party on its own initiative or on the demand of not less than one-third of the total membership represented at the preceding Party Congress. An Extraordinary Congress shall be convened within two months and is considered properly constituted if not less than one half of the total Party membership is represented at it.

The rates of representation at a Party Congress are determined by the Central Committee.

32. Should the Central Committee of the Party fail to convene an Extraordinary Congress within the period specified in Article 31, the organizations which demanded it have the right to form an Organizing Committee which shall enjoy the powers of the Central Committee of the Party in respect of the convocation of the Extraordinary Congress.

33. The Congress:

(a) hears and approves the reports of the Central Committee, of the Central Auditing Commission, and of the other central organizations;

(b) reviews, amends and endorses the Programme and the Rules of the Party;

(c) determines the line of the Party in matters of home and foreign policy, and examines and decides the most important questions of Party and state life, of communist construction;

(d) elects the Central Committee and the Central Auditing Commission.

34. The number of members to be elected to the Central Committee and to the Central Auditing Commission is determined by the Congress. In the event of vacancies occurring in the Central Committee, they are filled from among the alternate members of the CC CPSU.

35. In the interim between congresses, the Central Committee of the Communist Party of the Soviet Union directs the activities of the Party, the local Party bodies, selects and appoints leading functionaries, directs the work of central government bodies and public organizations of working people, sets up various Party organs, institutions and enterprises, and directs their activities, appoints the editors of the central newspapers and journals operating under its control, and distributes the funds of the Party budget and controls its execution.

The Central Committee represents the CPSU in its relations with other Parties.

36. The Central Auditing Commission of the CPSU supervises the observance of the established procedure of handling of affairs, the work done on considering the letters, applications and com-

plaints from the working people in the Party's central organs, and audits the correctness of execution of the Party budget, including the payment, collection and accounting of Party dues, and also the financial and economic activities of the enterprises and offices of the CPSU Central Committee.

37. The CC CPSU shall hold not less than one plenary meeting every six months. Alternate members of the Central Committee shall attend its plenary meetings with consultative voice.

38. The Central Committee of the Communist Party of the Soviet Union elects a Politbureau to direct the work of the Party between plenary meetings of the CC and a Secretariat to direct current work, chiefly the selection of cadres and the verification of the fulfilment of Party decisions. The Central Committee elects the General Secretary of the CC CPSU.

39. The Central Committee of the Communist Party of the Soviet Union organizes the Party Control Committee of the CC.

The Party Control Committee of the CC CPSU:

(a) verifies the observance of Party discipline by members and candidate members of the CPSU, and takes action against Communists who violate the Programme and the Rules of the Party, and Party or state discipline, and against violators of Party ethics;

(b) considers appeals against decisions of Central Committees of the Communist Parties of the Union Republics or of territorial and regional Party committees to expel members from the Party or impose penalties upon them.

40. Between Party congresses the CPSU Central Committee can convene, if the need arises, an All-Union Party Conference to discuss topical questions concerning Party policy. The order of holding an All-Union Party Conference is determined by the CC CPSU.

V. Republican, Territorial, Regional, Area, City and District Organizations of the Party

41. The Republican, territorial, regional, area, city and district Party organizations and their committees take guidance in their activities from the Programme and the Rules of the CPSU, conduct

all work for the implementation of Party policy and organize the fulfilment of the directives of the CC CPSU within the Republics, territories, regions, areas, cities and districts concerned.

42. The basic duties of Republican, territorial, regional, area, city and district Party organizations, and of their leading bodies, are:

(a) political and organizational work among the masses, mobilization of the Communists and all working people for the fulfilment of the tasks of communist construction, the acceleration of socio-economic development on the basis of scientific and technological progress, for raising the effectiveness of social production and labour productivity, improving the quality of output, for the fulfilment of state plans and socialist obligations, ensurance of the steady improvement of the material and cultural standards of the working people;

(b) organization of ideological work, propaganda of Marxism-Leninism, promotion of the communist awareness of the working people, guidance of the local press, radio and television, and control over the activities of scientific, cultural and educational institutions;

(c) guidance of Soviets of People's Deputies, trade union, YCL, cooperative and other public organizations through the Communists working in them, and increasingly broader enlistment of working people in the activities of these organizations, development of the initiative and activity of the masses as an essential condition for the further in-depth development of socialist democracy;

(d) strict observance of the Leninist principles and methods of management, the consolidation of the Leninist style in Party work, in all spheres of state and economic management, securing the unity of ideological, organizational and economic activities, the strengthening of socialist legality, state and labour discipline, order and organization in all sectors;

(e) conducting the cadres policy, education of the personnel in the spirit of communist ideology, moral purity, a high sense of responsibility to the Party and the people for the work entrusted to them;

(f) organization of various institutions and enterprises of the Party within the bounds of their Republic, territory, region, area, city or district, and guidance of their activities; distribution of Party funds within the given organization; systematic information of the higher Party body and accountability to it for their work.

Leading Bodies of Republican, Territorial and Regional Party Organizations

43. The highest body of Republican, territorial and regional Party organizations is the Congress of the Communist Party of the Union Republic and the respective territorial or regional Party conference, and in the interim between them the Central Committee of the Communist Party of the Union Republic and the territorial or regional committee.

44. A regular Congress of the Communist Party of the Union Republic is convened by the Central Committee of the Communist Party at least once in five years. Regular territorial and regional Party conferences are convened by the respective territorial or regional committees once every two–three years. Extraordinary congresses and conferences are convened by decision of the Central Committee of the Communist Party of the Union Republic, or territorial or regional committees, or on the demand of one-third of the total membership of the organizations belonging to the Republican, territorial or regional Party organization.

The rates of representation at congresses of the Communist Parties of the Union Republics and at territorial and regional conferences are determined by the respective Party committees.

Congresses of the Communist Parties of the Union Republics, and territorial and regional conferences, hear the reports of the Central Committee of the Communist Party of the Union Republic, or the respective territorial or regional committees, and of the auditing commission, discuss at their own discretion other matters of Party, economic and cultural development, and elect the Central Committee of the Communist Party of the Union Republic, the territorial or regional committee, the auditing commission and the delegates to the Congress of the CPSU.

Between congresses of the Communist Parties of the Union Republics the Central Committees of the Communist Parties can convene, if the need arises, Republican Party conferences to discuss topical questions concerning Party organizations' activities. The order of holding them is determined by the Central Committees of the Communist Parties of the Union Republics.

45. The Central Committees of the Communist Parties of the Union Republics and the territorial and regional committees elect bureaus, which also include secretaries of the committees. The secretaries must have a Party standing of not less than five years. The

plenary meetings of the committees confirm the heads of departments of these committees, the chairmen of Party control commissions, editors of Party newspapers and journals.

The Central Committees of the Communist Parties of the Union Republics, territorial and regional Party committees set up secretariats to examine current business and verify the execution of decisions.

46. The plenary meetings of the Central Committees of the Communist Parties of the Union Republics and territorial and regional committees shall be convened at least once every four months.

47. The Central Committees of the Communist Parties of the Union Republics and the territorial and regional committees direct the area, city and district Party organizations, inspect their work and regularly hear reports of the respective Party committees.

Party organizations in Autonomous Republics, and in autonomous and other regions forming part of a Union Republic or a territory function under the guidance of the Central Committees of the Communist Parties of the Union Republics or the respective territorial committees.

Leading Bodies of Area, City and District (Urban and Rural) Party Organizations

48. The highest body of an area, city or district Party organization is the area, city and district Party conference or the general meeting of Communists convened by the area, city or district committee once in two–three years, and the extraordinary conference convened by decision of the respective committee or on the demand of one-third of the total membership of the Party organization concerned.

The area, city or district conference (general meeting) hears reports of the committee and auditing commission, discusses at its own discretion other questions of Party, economic and cultural development, and elects the area, city and district committee, the auditing commission and delegates to the regional and territorial conference or the Congress of the Communist Party of the Union Republic.

The rates of representation to the area, city or district conference are determined by the respective Party committee.

49. The area, city or district committee elects a bureau, including the committee secretaries, and confirms the appointment of heads of committee departments, chairman of the Party commission and newspaper editors. The secretaries of the area, city and district committees must have a Party standing of at least five years. The committee secretaries are confirmed by the respective regional or territorial committee, or the Central Committee of the Communist Party of the Union Republic.

50. The area, city and district committee organizes the primary Party organizations, directs their work, regularly hears reports concerning the work of Party organizations, and keeps a register of Communists.

51. The plenary meeting of the area, city and district committee is convened at least once in three months.

VI. Primary Party Organizations

52. Primary Party organizations are the basis of the Party.

Primary Party organizations are formed at the places of work of Party members—in factories, state farms and other enterprises, collective farms, units of the Armed Forces, offices, educational establishments, etc., wherever there are not less than three Party members. Should the necessity arise, primary Party organizations may also be organized on the residential principle.

In individual cases, with the sanction of the regional, territorial committee, or the Central Committee of the Communist Party of the Union Republic, Party organizations may be formed within the framework of several enterprises that form a production association and are located, as a rule, on the territory of one or several districts in the same city.

53. At enterprises, collective farms and institutions with over 50 Party members and candidate members of the CPSU, shop, sectional, farm, team, departmental, etc., Party organizations may be formed as units of the general primary Party organization with the sanction of the district, city or area committee.

Within shop, sectional, etc., organizations and also within primary Party organizations having less than 50 members and candidate members, Party groups may be formed in the teams and other production units.

54. The highest organ of the primary Party organization is the

Party meeting, which is convened at least once a month. In Party organizations with shop or departmental Party organizations, both general and shop or departmental meetings are convened at least once in two months.

In large Party organizations with a membership of more than 300 Communists, a general Party meeting is convened when necessary at times fixed by the Party committee or on the demand of a number of shop or departmental Party organizations.

55. For the conduct of current business the primary, shop or departmental Party organization elects a bureau for the term of two or three years. The number of its members is fixed by the Party meeting. Primary, shop and departmental Party organizations with less than 15 Party members do not elect a bureau. Instead, they elect a secretary and deputy secretary of the Party organization. Elections in these organizations are held every year.

Secretaries of primary, shop and departmental Party organizations must have a Party standing of at least one year.

Primary Party organizations with less than 150 Party members shall have, as a rule, no salaried functionaries released from their regular work.

56. In large factories and offices with more than 300 members and candidate members of the Party, and in exceptional cases in factories and offices with over 100 Communists, by virtue of special production conditions and territorial disconnection, subject to the approval of the regional committee, Communist Party of the Union Republic, Party committees may be formed, the shop and departmental organizations being granted the status of primary Party organizations.

In Party organizations of collective farms, state farms and other agricultural enterprises Party committees may be formed if they have 50 Communists.

In Party organizations with over 500 Communists Party committees may be formed in large shops in individual cases with the sanction of the regional committee, territorial committee or Central Committee of the Communist Party of the Union Republic, and the Party organizations of production sections may be granted the status of primary Party organizations.

The Party committees are elected for the term of 2–3 years. Their numerical composition is fixed by the general Party meeting or conference.

Party committees, Party bureaus, secretaries of primary, shop or departmental Party organizations systematically inform Communists of their work at Party meetings.

57. Party committees of primary Party organizations with more than 1,000 Communists may be granted, with the sanction of the Central Committee of the Communist Party of the Union Republic, the powers of a district Party committee in matters of admission of new members to the CPSU, keeping a register of members and candidate members of the Party and consideration of personal cases of Communists.

These organizations may elect enlarged Party committees within which bureaus are formed to guide day-to-day work.

58. In its activities the primary Party organization takes guidance from the Programme and the Rules of the CPSU. It is the political nucleus of a work collective, it conducts its work directly among the working people, rallies them round the Party, organizes them to fulfil tasks of communist construction, takes an active part in implementing the Party's cadres policy.

The primary Party organization:

(a) admits new members to the CPSU;

(b) educates Communists in a spirit of loyalty to the Party cause, ideological staunchness and communist ethics;

(c) organizes the study by Communists of Marxist-Leninist theory in close connection with the practice of communist construction and combats any manifestations of bourgeois ideology, revisionism and dogmatism, backward views and moods;

(d) takes care of raising the vanguard role of Communists in the sphere of labour and socio-political activities, and their exemplary behaviour in everyday life, and hears reports from members and candidate members of the CPSU about their fulfilment of the duties required by the Rules and Party assignments;

(e) acts as the organizer of the working people for the solving of tasks of economic and social development, heads the socialist emulation movement for the fulfilment of state plans and undertakings, the intensification of production, the raising of labour productivity and quality of products, the introduction on a broad scale into production of achievements of science and technology, of advanced experience, rallies the working people to disclose untapped resources, works to achieve the rational, economical use of material, labour and financial resources, shows concern for the protection and increase of public wealth, for improving conditions of people's work and daily life;

(f) conducts agitational and propaganda work, educates the working people in the spirit of devotion to the ideas of communism, Soviet patriotism and peoples' friendship, helps them to cultivate high-standard political culture and enhances their social activity and responsibility;

(g) works to foster in Communists and all working people the habits of taking part in socialist self-government, ensures the enhancement of the role of the work collective in running the affairs of enterprises and institutions, directs the work of trade union, YCL and other public organizations;

(h) on the basis of extensive spread of criticism and self-criticism, combats cases of bureaucracy, parochialism, departmentalism, violations of state, labour and production discipline, thwarts attempts to deceive the state, acts against negligence, waste and extravagance, strives to vindicate a sobriety.

59. Primary Party organizations of enterprises of industry, transport, communication, construction, material and technical supplies, trade, public catering, communal and other services, collective and state farms and other agricultural enterprises, design organizations, drafting offices, research institutes, educational establishments, cultural and medical institutions, enjoy the right to control the work of the administration.

The Party organizations at ministries, state committees, and other central or local government, economic agencies and departments exercise control of how the apparatus fulfils the directives of the Party and government and observes Soviet laws. They must actively promote improvement of the apparatus, the election, placing and education of its personnel, enhance their sense of responsibility for work entrusted to them, for the development of the branch, the servicing of the population, promote state discipline, firmly combat bureaucracy and red tape, inform the appropriate Party bodies in good time on shortcomings in the work of the respective offices and individuals, regardless of what posts the latter may occupy.

Note. Primary Party organizations may set up commissions to exercise the right to control the administration's activities, and the work of the apparatus in separate avenues of production activity.

VII. The Party and the State and Public Organizations

60. The CPSU, acting in the framework of the Constitution of the USSR, exercises political guidance over the state and public organizations, directs and coordinates their work.

The Party organizations and the Communists who work in state and public organizations ensure that these organizations should in full measure exercise their powers under the Constitution, the rights and duties under the Rules, and draw the working people on a wide scale into management and the solution of political, economic and social questions.

Party organizations are not a substitute for the government, trade union, cooperative and other public organizations, and do not allow the mixing of the functions of the Party and other organs.

61. Party groups are formed at congresses, conferences, meetings convened by state and public organizations, as well as at the elected organs of these organizations, having at least three Party members. The task of these groups is to carry out the Party's policy in the corresponding non-Party organizations, increase the influence of Communists on the state of affairs in these organizations, promote the democratic norms of their activities, strengthen Party and state discipline, combat red tape, and check up on the fulfilment of Party and government directives.

62. The work of the Party groups within non-Party organizations is directed by a corresponding Party organ: the CPSU Central Committee, the Central Committee of the Communist Party of the Union Republic, territorial, regional, area, city, district Party committee.

VIII. The Party and the YCL

63. The Leninist Young Communist League of the Soviet Union is an independently acting social and political organization of young people, an active helper and reserve of the Party. The YCL helps the Party to educate the youth in the communist spirit, draw it into the work of building a new society, into the management of state and public affairs, to mould a generation of harmoniously de-

veloped people who are ready for labour and defence of the Soviet Motherland.

64. The YCL organizations must be active levers in the implementation of Party directives in all spheres of production and public life. They enjoy the right of broad initiative in discussing and submitting to the appropriate Party organizations questions related to the work of enterprises, collective farms, offices and educational establishments, take a direct part in solving them, especially if they pertain to work, everyday life, teaching and educating of young people.

65. The YCL conducts its activities under the guidance of the Communist Party of the Soviet Union. The work of the local YCL organizations is directed and controlled by the appropriate Republican, territorial, regional, area, city and district Party organizations.

In their communist educational work among the youth, in rallying it for the fulfilment of specific tasks of production and social life, local Party bodies and primary Party organizations rely on the support of the YCL organizations, uphold their useful initiatives, give every assistance in their activity.

66. Members of the YCL who have been admitted into the CPSU cease to belong to the YCL the moment they join the Party, provided they are not members of elected YCL organs and do not work as YCL functionaries.

IX. Party Organizations in the Armed Forces

67. Party organizations in the Armed Forces take guidance in their work from the Programme and the Rules of the CPSU and operate on the basis of instructions approved by the Central Committee. They carry out the policy of the Party in the Armed Forces, rally servicemen round the Communist Party, educate them in the spirit of Marxism-Leninism and boundless loyalty to the socialist homeland, actively further the unity of the army and the people, take care to raise the combat preparedness of troops, work for the strengthening of military discipline, rally servicemen to carry out the tasks of combat training and political education and acquire skill in the use of new material and weapons, and to irreproachably per-

form their military duty and the orders and instructions of the command.

68. The guidance of Party work in the Armed Forces is exercised by the Central Committee of the CPSU through political bodies. The Chief Political Administration of the Soviet Army and Navy functions as a department of the CC CPSU.

The chiefs of the political administrations of military districts and fleets, and chiefs of the political departments of armies, flotillas and formations must be Party members of five years' standing.

69. The Party organizations and political bodies of the Armed Forces maintain close contact with local Party committees, and keep them informed about political work in the military units. The secretaries of military Party organizations and chiefs of political bodies participate in the work of local Party committees.

X. Party Funds

70. The funds of the Party and its organizations are derived from membership dues, incomes from Party enterprises and other revenue.

The manner in which Party funds are to be used is decided upon by the CPSU Central Committee.

71. The monthly membership dues for Party members and candidate members are as follows:

Monthly earnings	Dues	
up to 70 roubles	10 kopeks	
from 71 to 100 roubles	20 kopeks	
from 101 to 150 roubles	1.0 per cent	of the
from 151 to 200 roubles	1.5 per cent	monthly
from 201 to 250 roubles	2.0 per cent	earnings
from 251 to 300 roubles	2.5 per cent	
over 300 roubles	3.0 per cent	

72. An entrance fee of 2 per cent of the monthly earnings is paid on admission to the Party as a candidate member.

About the Authors

ROY D. LAIRD is a professor of political science and Soviet and East European studies at the University of Kansas. He received his Ph.D. from the University of Washington in 1956. Most of his books, articles, and book chapters have dealt with various aspects of Soviet agricultural affairs. He is the founder of the International Conference on Soviet and East European Agriculture. His most recent book is *The Politburo: Demographic Trends, Gorbachev, and the Future,* Westview Press, 1986.

BETTY A. LAIRD is an independent research analyst who works in the fields of Soviet studies and Kansas history. Her formal education includes a B.A. (cum laude) in theatre and English from Hastings College and postgraduate courses in Russian history and language, English literature, and statistics.

0011259396